P9-EDU-758

CANADIAN LITERARY PROSE

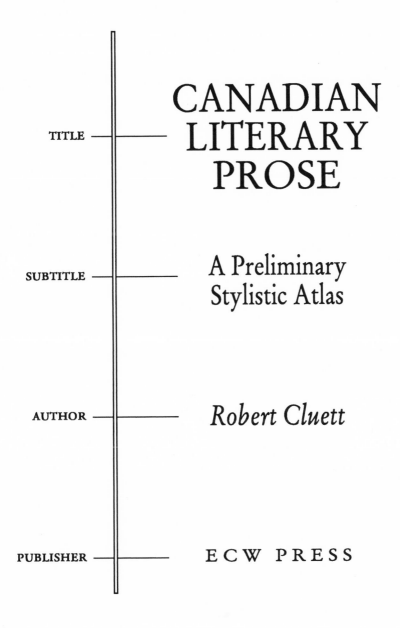

TITLE

CANADIAN LITERARY PROSE

SUBTITLE

A Preliminary
Stylistic Atlas

AUTHOR

Robert Cluett

PUBLISHER

ECW PRESS

CANADIAN CATALOGUING IN PUBLICATION DATA

Cluett, Robert

Canadian literary prose

Includes index.
ISBN 1-55022-096-9 (bound) ISBN 1-55022-098-5 (pbk.)

1. Canadian fiction (English) — 20th century — History and criticism.*
2. Novelists, Canadian (English) — 20th century.* 3. Style, Literary. I. Title.

PS8187.C58 1990   c813'255.5'255.09   c89-094669-8
L8690   PR9192.5.C58 1990

This book has been published with the assistance of a grant from
the Canadian Federation for the Humanities, using funds provided
by the Social Sciences and Humanities Research Council of Canada.
Additional grants have been provided by the Ontario Arts Council
and The Canada Council.

Design and imaging by ECW Type & Art, Oakville, Ontario.
Printed and bound by The Porcupine's Quill, Erin, Ontario.

Distributed by Butterworths Canada Ltd.
75 Clegg Road, Markham, Ontario L6G 1A1

Published by ECW PRESS
307 Coxwell Avenue, Toronto, Ontario M4L 3B5

ACKNOWLEDGMENTS

Many thanks: 1) To the Graduate Programme in English, York University, for underwriting Research Assistants to this project, the York Computer Inventory of Prose Style, to the extent of some $30,000 since 1969; 2) To The Canada Council (predecessor to the SSHRCC) for some $21,000 in supporting grants; 3) To the Faculty of Arts Minor Research Grants Fund for $2,400 in support of a Research Assistant for the summer of 1987; 4) To the Master of Winters College, York University, who since 1972 has provided space for the project and for its miles of printout.

The many helping hands that the project has employed since 1969 are listed in Appendix B. To all of them, thanks again. Particular thanks, however, go to Jerry Carpenter, our indefatigable programmer, to Suzanne Ives, who did all the preliminary lexical work for the analysis of *Duddy Kravitz*, and to Linda Blom and Louise MacDonald Drescher, both of whom have put in nearly four years on the project. Without their outstanding work as syntactic and lexical analysts of the texts scrutinized in this book, I would have had an additional twelve to eighteen months getting ready to write. Particular thanks, also, to Lydia Rett and Linda Revie, who helped edit the book's final proofs, and to Jack David, who has been helpful throughout in his double capacity of both editor and publisher.

I owe an incalculable debt of gratitude to Louis T. Milic for introducing me to the mysteries of his method in 1966 and 1967 and for his helpful interest in the York Inventory from its beginnings. Scholars in other institutions who have used the materials of the York Inventory and its programs include, in addition to Professor Milic, Don Ross (University of Minnesota), Michael Farringdon (University College Swansea), and Ian Lancashire (University of Toronto); I am grateful to each and all of them for helpful suggestions and useful feedback.

Finally, I acknowledge with deep gratitude the helpfulness of Clara Thomas, Eli Mandel, and John Lennox in introducing me to the literature of Canada in the early 1970s, and that of Frank Davey in giving me a highly perspicacious set of responses to the second draft of this book.

Plaudits for such virtues as the book may have should be extended to all those named above. For its shortcomings, alas, I must reserve sole credit to myself.

R.C.
Wellington, Ontario
June, 1989

TABLE OF CONTENTS

LIST OF TABLES

LIST OF FIGURES

SECTION ——|—— # Place & Language

Part 1.0

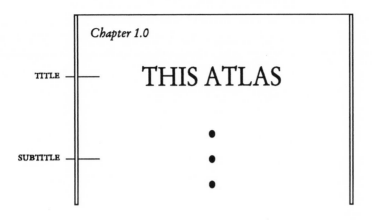

Chapter 1.0

TITLE

THIS ATLAS

•

•

•

SUBTITLE

THE STUDY

This atlas is both a resource and, to a lesser extent, a delivery and refinement of critical findings from the York University Computer Inventory of Prose Style. As a resource, it makes available extensive linguistic data on the 53 samples from Canadian texts listed in Table 1.1 — 27 fiction and 26 nonfiction. These were selected, sampled, translated into a computer syntactic code, and computer-analyzed between 1975 and 1981. The samples were updated to the latest (1986) revision of the York Inventory syntactic code, described later in this chapter, in 1986–87. A description of the sampling procedure, of the translating of the samples into the three-digit syntactic code and of the manipulations performed by our various computer programs has been published (*Prose Style*), and I shall not trouble my reader or publisher with recapitulation of material already available, though we give a brief summary of the programs in Appendix C.

The book is called an *Atlas*, even though it is somewhat less comprehensive in scope than its sister volumes in geography. There are good reasons for use of the title. One of the book's primary interests is in fact an interest in place — places called Canada, Great Britain, and America — and its findings are delivered in a form that is quantitative and spatial. Though the book does offer a few modest insights, its intentions are essentially compilative in character; the data are put forward not as a means to bend readers of the book to my interpretive views but as facts that readers might find useful on their own. Its principal affinities are with other forms of compilative scholarship: bibliographies, dictionaries, concordances, and atlases. The reader who wishes to plumb the syntactic sources of Laurence's remarkable simplicity or the reader who wishes to consider the distinctive peculiarities of Grove's use of the English verb system may now conveniently do so with this book, given only a few current grammatical terms, plus some very basic grammatical knowledge. A glossary of terms is included in Appendix D.

If we were starting the research for this in 1989, I would opt for a base of 35 to 50 samples on each side — I would include on the nonfiction side Mavis Gallant, June Callwood, Eli Mandel, Barbara Amiel, Jack Granatstein, Kenneth McNaught, plus others. On the fiction side I would add more Callaghan, more Hood, more Laurence, more Davies, some Munro, some Engel, plus several of our recently emerged *luminati*: Wiebe, Kroetsch, Bowering, Findley at least, no doubt others as well. However, continuous updating is impossible without continuous new funding, and in an ongoing project like this inventory one must stop and deliver findings at appropriate points. We have reached such a point. We have far more data than we have conclusions; there are things to say and new vistas to be considered.

Whatever the biases and omissions — and there will be some in any selection from any canon — this book makes available for the first time a large amount of systematically analyzed linguistic data on objectively chosen samples from a number of recognized Canadian writers. Those data are presented not just in Canadian terms but together with similar data on 40 samples from major figures in British and American literature, writing over the last 200 years, mainly the period 1900–75, and in comparison with the 1976 and 1982 York studies. The data can be viewed *en grosso*, as they will be in the remaining chapters of Part I, to generate and test hypotheses about time, genre, and place. They can also be used to consider insistent propensities in a particular text or a particular writer, as they will be in the four chapters of Part II. By the end, we shall still be a long way from exhausting the myriad possibilities inherent in the syntactic information displayed in Appendix A; that task is left for the other users of this book and of the York Inventory. The book is not an attempt to be the last linguistic word on Canadian literary prose; its claims are much more modest than that. But it does do some things, mainly two: 1) it makes available its data in convenient form (computer printouts are impenetrably cryptic for the non-specialist, and their size makes comparison difficult),[1] and 2) it offers a few demonstrations of some of the critical ends to which a close reading of those data, together with a close reading of the texts, might be put. The texts that are the focus of the study are listed in Table 1.1: the Anglo-American comparison texts are listed in Table 1.2. The 1976 study was published in *Prose Style and Critical Reading*; some findings of the 1982 study are published here for the first time.

TABLE 1.1

Canadian Writers & Works

Richardson, *Wacousta*	Strachan, *Documents and Opinions*
Connor, *Man from Glengarry*	MacKenzie, *1837*
Duncan, *The Imperialist*	Moodie, *Roughing it in The Bush*
Montgomery, *Anne of Green Gables*	Howe, *Poems and Essays*
Leacock, *Sunshine Sketches* (x 2)	McGee, *Speeches and Addresses*
Ostenso, *Wild Geese*	Pearson, *Mike*
de la Roche, *Jalna*	Diefenbaker, *One Canada*
Callaghan, *A Native Argosy*	Dewart, *The Bible under*
/*Strange Fugitive*	*Higher Criticism*
Grove, *Fruits of the Earth*	Creighton, *Dominion of the North*
Ross, *As for Me and My House*	Callaghan, *That Summer in Paris*
MacLennan, *Two Solitudes*	Galbraith, *New Industrial State*
MacLennan, *Each Man's Son*	McLuhan, *The Gutenberg Galaxy*
Lowry, *Under the Volcano*	McLuhan, *Understanding Media*
Mitchell, *Who Has Seen the Wind*	Layton, *Engagements*
Buckler, *The Mountain and The Valley*	Frye, *Fables of Identity*
Wiseman, *The Sacrifice*	Woodcock, *Rejection of Politics*
Richler, *Duddy Kravitz*	Woodcock, *Lost Eurydice*
Cohen, *The Favourite Game*	Davies, *A Voice from the Attic*
Laurence, *The Stone Angel*	Berton, *The Smug Minority*
Hood, *The Swing in the Garden*	Berton, *The Last Spike*
Davies, *Fifth Business*	Dobbs, *Reading the Time*
Davies, *The Manticore*	Newman, *A Nation Divided*
Atwood, *Surfacing*	Fulford, *Crisis at the Victory*
Atwood, *The Edible Woman*	Richler, *Hunting Tigers*
Atwood, *Life Before Man*	Stewart, *Shrug*
Godfrey, *The New Ancestors*	Atwood, *Survival*

TABLE I.2

Anglo-American Writers & Works

Hawthorne, *Tanglewood Tales*
Howells, *The Rise of Silas Lapham*
Twain, *Tales*
James, *Washington Square*
Fitzgerald, *Tender Is the Night*
Steinbeck, *Cannery Row*
West, *Miss Lonelyhearts*
Faulkner, *As I Lay Dying*
Nabokov, *Lolita*
Roth, *Portnoy's Complaint*
Dickens, *Bleak House*
Trollope, *The Warden*
Stevenson, *Kidnapped*
Conrad, *The Secret Agent*
Joyce, *Portrait of the Artist*
Lawrence, *Lady Chatterly's Lover*
Woolf, *To the Lighthouse*
Forster, *Passage to India*
Orwell, *1984*
Burgess, *MF*

Cooper, *Notions of the Americans*
Jefferson, *A Summary View . . .*
Thoreau, *Walden*
Mencken, *A Mencken Crestomathy*
Stein, *Paris France*
Hemingway, *Death in the Afternoon*
Fitzgerald, *The Crack-up*
Wilson, *Axel's Castle*
Stone, Columns (*IF Stone's Weekly*)
Didion, *Slouching toward Bethlehem*
Huxley, *Evolution and Ethics*
Arnold, *A Democratic Education*
Conrad, *Prefaces*
Joyce, *Critical Writings*
Woolf, *The Common Reader, I*
Forster, *Aspects of the Novel*
Waugh, *A Little Learning*
Orwell, *Collected Essays*
Burgess, *The Novel Now*
Steiner, *Language and Silence*

THEORY & ASSUMPTIONS

We live in what seems to have been a great age of theory: the shifting interests of people in graduate schools are a testament. Thirty years ago, our graduate students tended to speak of the major writers of the English tradition — from Chaucer, Shakespeare, and Milton up to figures as recent as Hardy perhaps, or Joyce or Yeats. Over time, that changed to the point where, by the late 1970s, many Canadian graduate students tended to concentrate not only on Canadian writers but on living Canadian poets and novelists. This more recent focus of interest remains strong, but it now goes hand-in-hand with — indeed, is often displaced by — an interest in some kind of current critical theory: Marxist, feminist, deconstructionist, or a combination of two or more of these.[2] What this book is about has no *a priori* conflict with any of these perspectives. No *ism* that pretends to deal with linguistic and social artifacts — i.e. with texts — need feel threatened by the systematic assembly of a large body of factual material about the language of objectively chosen samples[3] from texts of demonstrated critical interest. Indeed, one would hope that such an assembly holds promise for enrichment and verification of much that theory might bring to text and of much close reading that is based on fragmentary and highly selective textual choice.

The matter of enrichment is straightforward. Modes of literary criticism for the last 300+ years — including deconstruction — have insistently focused on words and on aesthetic structures, eschewing the analysis of syntactic structures even though the syntax of a work or of a writer may have great potential importance for reasons involving both aesthetics and meaning. And verification in criticism as in the law courts can encourage, perhaps even reward, truthful and responsible utterance. For example, one could analyze what is arguably the most famous single sentence in English prose fiction, the opening sentence of *Pride and Prejudice*, and come to the conclusion that Austen's language and method are indirect, that they embody the preceding century's interest in generalization, that they show a far keener interest in human action than in human attributes. What assurance have we, apart from Austen's admitted writership, that the immortal sentence in question is representative of how Austen generally wrote? Not much. But a glimpse at the Austen data in *Prose Style and Critical Reading* confirms that the sentence is indeed as typical as any single sentence from any writer could be.[4] Such knowledge is a comfort to the reader who would like to see more of a text than a given critic might often choose to show us or even to consider.[5]

Beneath any critical undertaking there lies a tissue of theoretical and practical assumptions, sometimes coherent, sometimes not, and it is useful if the critic is able to make explicit just what those assumptions are. In this case they are few and not of staggering complexity. Beyond the existence of style itself and the existence of complex interconnexions between the language of literature and the language of the society that produces it, the main assumptions of this study are as follows.

1) The English language, in all its venues, changes over time.

2) Oral English varies substantially from place to place, and geographical variation can manifest itself not only in speech but in literary prose.

3) In accordance with variation of relationship between language user (writer) and audience (reader), the language has varying levels of formality, which in turn signal differing tenor relationships between writer and audience.

4) Literary genres "bend" the language in the direction of their own conventions (Brainerd). Most conspicuously, those who would communicate by means of a sonnet will have their language (strongly though perhaps not infallibly) bent in the direction of fourteen-line utterance in iambic pentameter.

5) Despite constraints of time, place, tenor, and genre, the style of any given writer *tends* to remain distinctive in crucial and identifiable respects.[6] Though a writer may be girt round with the bonds of the language as given, yet will the writer's own identity work against those bonds at a number of conscious and unconscious points.

6) Language is the medium of literature, and the critic who undertakes literary interpretation while despising or ignoring any aspect of language risks a biased or fragmentary reading. Such readings may, from time to time, need augmenting.[7]

7) Language is more than just its words, and the history or the demography of a language — even, as here, the literary dialect of a language — must extend its compass beyond vocabulary to include other linguistic features important to meaning and form; in the case of this work, syntax, or grammar.

8) The conscious and unconscious linguistic choices made by one writer or by a group of associated writers can have substantial interpretive importance. This of course assumes that there is a "centre" to the text, to be interpreted. Anyone's ability to reach that centre or grasp it whole is, to me, a matter moot at best. But as a convention of proceeding I am prepared to assume that at least in some Platonic sense there is a centre.

Though the first four of these assumptions above may seem more germane to the remaining chapters of Part i and the second four to the particular treatments of writers in Part ii, all eight are in some way present in the book's every utterance.

Placing these assumptions in the general context of critical theory and its history is not difficult: they are by and large the assumptions of classical North American linguistics,[8] the linguistics of Bloomfield, Jesperson, and Hockett. To a point, I would plead guilty to one semeiologist's charge:

> Even the most workmanlike investigation of linguistic structure aims at revealing the system of relations assumed to be immanent in the data. This usually results in a description which is internally consistent and in full compliance with the admonition of Ockham's razor; such as one might, for instance, find in a good grammar book of a language analyzed in that manner, serving the ends of pedagogy and general information. (Shapiro 11)

If one is a teacher by trade and is also into teleology, these are not wholly despicable ends. They are, after all, the ends of my first three chapters. I would not even quarrel with what the writer goes on to say:

> A truly interpretive analysis, however, aspires to an explanatory understanding that goes beyond the cataloguing of linguistic units and the rules of their combination. Its ultimate goal is re-cognition of the cognized relations embodied by the facts.

Nothing arguable there, I would say, unless cognition and cognized are specified as fully conscious on the part of the writer.

TERMS: *Writer/Author, Syntax/Grammar, Style/Form, Text/Interpretation*

Post-structuralist criticism has much affected literalness in the derivation of some of its terms. For example:

> When used [*author*] means ... the writer is seen as endowed with "authorial" attributes, such as full conscious control of the writing process and "authority" over the meaning of what has been written. (Roudiez 13)

Out of respect for this literal tendency, I shall try to avoid the term *author*, despite its lengthy service in practical criticism as a synonym for *writer*. Few of us, if any, have *authority* over our language or over the forms it takes, and our language-generating processes, especially the syntactic aspect of those processes, are much of the time not subjected to conscious control.

Grammar, sentence structure, discourse structure, syntax — these are often used in overlapping senses. *Grammatology*, the study specifically of that which is written (deriving from the Greek *Gram*), together with the widespread currency of the works of its progenitor, Jacques Derrida, has managed to cloud a lot of the associations that the word *grammar* has historically had — and perhaps rightfully so. *Grammar* is in any case often a suspect term, even more so than many other terms in linguistics. *Sentence structure* and *discourse structure* name something of what this book is about, but the book also considers more minute phenomena and more microscopically. No term will be wholly or universally satisfactory as a name for the general process of naming sequences and their constituents. *Syntax* is the term that I have chosen. *Syntax*, like *grammar*, has more than one sense, since as Halliday points out "it has come into present-day linguistics from two different sources and so . . . has two different meanings" (*Language*). Halliday goes on to say:

> On the one hand you have syntax in the context of semantics-syntactics-pragmatics, where it is defined in terms of a general theory of signs, on criteria which are drawn from outside language. On the other hand, there is the context in which you have semantics-grammar-phonetics, and then within grammar you have the division into syntax-morphology. This is a different sense of the term, where the criteria are within language itself; syntax is that part of the grammatical system which deals with the combination of words into sentences or phrases into sentences. (43–44)

It is in this latter sense that this book uses the term *syntax*: phrase-, clause-, and sentence-structure. How the lexical items (the lexemes) are literally *put* (Tax) *together* (Syn) to form meaningful utterances.

Form and *style* are also often used in overlapping senses. They are, often, after all, aspects of each other. Style is, in Meyer Schapiro's formulation:

> . . . the constant form — and sometimes the constant elements, qualities, and expression — in the art of an individual or group. The term is also applied to the whole activity of the individual or society, as in speaking of a "life-style" or "the style of a civilization." (25)

I should note before returning to Schapiro's definition later that he has placed *individual* style as primary and *group* style as secondary. *Form*, in Schapiro's sense, can be accidental or unique; *Style*, on the other hand, is systematic and recursive. Not all of the profession, by any means, has rallied to Schapiro's banner. Roman Jakobsen has characterized style as

> a marked — emotive or poetic — annex to the neutral, purely cognitive information. (72)

If one were so to restrict the term, one could not speak — as I have heard scientists speak — of the style of a proof in physics or mathematics. No less eminent a stylistician than Robert Adolph has also held himself aloof from the Schapironist camp:

> Both the "other aspects of the text" and its "contextual settings" exist inseparably in an ill-defined but crucial region between the linguistic facts of the text and the response of the reader, that is, his perception and interpretation of stylistic intentions. Style for most people lies just here, between texts and intuitive responses of readers . . . . ("Possibility" 439)

It is true that in this dark and setting part of time we are increasingly conscious of the process of projection — of what once was expressed by the maxim, "The evil lies in the eye of the beholder." However, to give a projective definition to style is to debase both the writer of the text and the critical act by confusing the text itself with its analysis or with interpretation, a problem not only in Adolph's version of stylistics but in something more recent, namely deconstruction generally.[9] Despite evident widespread willingness, as in Kristeva and Derrida, to accept key terms by way of literal etymological definitions, few seem willing to do this with the term *style*, derived originally from the Greek *stylos*, the stick with which Greek schoolboys marked their wax tablets. One recognized a tablet as belonging to a particular individual by the *style* of the writing, by the *stylos*. The concept was gradually enlarged to include not only the distinctiveness of an individual's graphology but the distinct style of expression in the language given graphological form. That is the sense in which *style* is used in this book, Schapiro's sense: the mark of the maker, whether the maker be an individual, a group, a whole society, or a combination thereof. Style, therefore, has an existence in the *propensities* of the individual, group, or society, and those propensities are visible only in the *text*, or in a body of texts.

Text, in this sense, is a stable entity. It is the interpretation of the text that is clearly unstable and always has been. The collective consciousness has a history, as does that of the individual, and the collective or individual return to a text has always produced new and often radically different interpretations. Interpretation is by its very nature biased and mutable, and all interpretation carries within it the seeds of reinterpretation. But some interpretation is better than others; William Cain summarizes one view on this question as follows:

> Fish is not simply suggesting that . . . readers differ, for he adds that after we identify the different readers, we then rank them. The "informed reader" is the fourth one, and "his experience of the sentence will be not only different from, but better than, his less-informed fellows." (53)

Fish, who seems to view with pride the "constraint" that is embodied in his somewhat arbitrary "construct" of the "informed reader" ("What Is" 146) has taxed stylistics on the grounds that "its arbitrariness insures that it will never fail" (117). He may be right to the extent that not all interpretive stylistics manages to touch us with the shock of recognition; like any other critical mode, it has produced stuff that is downright bad. But arbitrary it need not be — provided its practice retains the methodological rigor of other branches of linguistics. The interpretation of syntactic data should ultimately be as disciplined and as responsible to the phenomena (i.e. as non-arbitrary) as the interpretation of lexis. Syntactic "meanings," after all, are largely susceptible to the same processes of adducement and verification as lexical "meanings" are susceptible to: principally *source, collocation,* and *context,* considered over repeated instances. There are texts the syntax of which is not only important but so overwhelmingly resonant as to constitute a major element of the work's total meaning: the *Psalms,* James's *The Wings of the Dove,* Conrad's *Heart of Darkness,* Atwood's *Surfacing,* to name only four of many that could be named.

In "Interpreting the *Variorum*" Fish suggests that all bodies of assumption, no matter how "objective," are equally biasing in their effects on the critical process. Under this notion, the linguistic concept of the tagmeme is every bit as arbitrary as the assumption often encountered in the New Critics that a poem has no existence as an historical artifact but rather is only "an imperfect gesture in the direction of a perfect utterance" (Wolf). It is ridiculous to postulate or even to suggest such an equivalence of assumption between a linguistic and descriptive approach to a text and some other approach less defined in its disciplinary constraints and less widely accepted among a discipline's practitioners. The tagmeme — an intersection of function and structure — is such a basic grammatical notion and so demonstrable in any English language text that any linguist of any persuasion can accept it, at least as a convention of proceeding towards some kind of analysis. Similarly, terms identifying grammatical functions and constructs — terms like subject and complement, or prepositional phrase, relative clause and sentence — name units that *all* linguistics specialists could identify in a text, whatever differences they might have in assumption or theoretical persuasion. Among literary scholars, on the other hand, there is wide disagreement on questions such as self/trueself, the location of the "meaning" (in the text or in the reader), the possibility of such a thing as "deconstructing" a text, and even the relation of a text to its historical context.

Probably the best way to cope with piscine canards about interpretation of stylistic data is to get on with it, to get on with the descriptive process and then with the process of interpretation. But I cannot leave the question of theory without at least one reference to the relation between theory and practice. William E. Cain has expressed a view of this worth citing here:

> Many of the major theorists began by calling attention to failures in practice, unexamined assumptions in criticism, and misunderstandings that warp pedagogy. But these theorists have allowed their studies to acquire a momentum that has taken them away from pedagogical and critical realities. Theory has become a game of its own, one whose compensation in status and professional visibility is all too apparent. And as theory has turned into a self-contained field, its proponents have left behind those who do the basic teaching in composition, introduction to literature, and survey courses, and who do not instruct bright graduate students in seminars on Nietsche and Marx or Derrida and Foucault. (Cain 248)

I would hope that this book has more than a clearly defined theoretical basis; I would hope its material might be of some use to readers anywhere dealing with these texts for the second, the third, or even the tenth time.

Between the theory and the practice falls the shadow of method. That has already been thoroughly described (*Prose Style*), but there is some updating to be done. Exactly what our computer programs do is set forth briefly in Appendix C.

Though we examine lexis in the individual studies in Part II, the emphasis of the book and of the new material that it publishes is syntactic. Modern linguistics, occasionally aided by the computer or illuminated by the computer's limitations, has given us numerous grammatical models for the description of syntax. Some of these are essentially Cartesian, and rest on highly abstract and normative assumptions, such as Chomsky's transformational-generative model. Others are Baconian, and rest entirely on data-gathering (what Bacon himself called "the very straw and sweepings of the stable"), such as Charles C. Fries's structural model. Still others have been derived in Isaac Newton's way, their progenitors gathering *some* data, constructing an hypothesis, and then testing the hypothesis against further data and observations (Randall). Such methods have distinguished the work of Pike, Becker, and Young in the U.S.A., of Firth, Halliday, and Spencer in the U.K., and of Michael Gregory in Canada. Though the tagmemic grammar of Pike and his followers differs in many ways from the category-scale grammar of Firth and his, they share some important features: 1) They place language within a larger framework of behaviour and activity, and 2) they separately consider phonological, lexicogrammatical, and semantic layers as aspects of language, dividing the second of these layers into lexis and syntax.[10]

The *ideal* grammar for stylistic description and interpretation would yield full and systematic analysis of both the semantic and the lexicogrammatical layers. In short, it would give us information on lexis, on structure types such as clause, phrase, word (noun, verb, etc.), on function types such as subject, predicator, object, and complement, and on semantic types such as actor, action, agent, recipient. But the ideal is difficult of attainment, especially in a project as large as this one. Cost has been a major obstacle. Over the course of this book, we shall make direct reference to 130 York Inventory samples, indirect reference to perhaps 40 or 45 more. Those samples will represent roughly fourteen dozen works each with an average length of 90,000 words; they constitute a 600,000-word sampling of texts totalling 15,000,000 words. To undertake more minute or delicate analysis before computer-processing would have been staggeringly expensive in the late 1960s and the 1970s.

The type of computer-assisted research on which this book delivers findings had its beginnings roughly 25 years ago, with Louis Milic's landmark study of Swift. Milic considered word-classes and word class sequences alone, proceeding through Swift and several control writers with a version of Fries's 1952 grammar that consisted of 24 enumerated word classes, each represented by a different two-digit code for computer processing. The York Inventory was begun in 1970 with a much expanded (98-slot) version of that Fries-Milic taxonomy: though the taxonomy remained largely a grammar of word-classes and strings, the addition of a third digit to the computer coding enabled the researchers to have much more flexibility than was at the disposal of the system's originator. Over time, we have expanded and refined the taxonomy to enable it better to yield information about both structures and functions. With the present version, we can do much more than we could even as recently as 1981, especially with respect to the analysis of clause types and of clause distributions.

The functional refinements in the grammar yield information largely about the phrase level of structure. We can now obtain functional information on noun phrases, verb phrases, and prepositional phrases. Relative clauses used restrictively (i.e. used as post-head qualifiers in noun phrases) are tagged. At the clause level, we can develop accurate inferences as to the distribution of structure types that fill subject function (nouns, pronouns, pattern markers), and the analysis of predicators remains very thorough (active / passive, finite / nonfinite, tense-marked / non-tense-marked). The coding now also gives accurate counts of additioned independent clauses, as in compound sentences. All of these changes have enhanced a system that even before them could yield considerable information.

Our latest revision of the Milic's taxonomy alters the coding published in 1976 by adding new third digits to the following word-class categories for the purposes indicated:

Noun (01) and Pronoun (11) — Added categories for Verb object (018, 118) and prepositional phrase completive (019, 119).

Relative Pronoun (43) — Added category 433 (Relative for restrictive clause) and changed category 431 to non-restrictive only.

Preposition (51) — Changed 511 to indicate that the word headed a noun-modifying phrase, and added category 514 to indicate an adverbially used phrase (Adjunct or Adverbial at clause rank; Modifier at phrase rank with Adverbs and Adjectives).

Coordinator (41) — Totally reorganized the system to focus not on what coordinators were used but on whether coordinators linked words/phrases or linked clauses. The full elaboration of the revised coding is given in Table 1.3.

The first three classes were changed in the interest of gaining more functional precision. The fourth change was made after long study of 18th-century texts, which suggested that the compound sentence did for some 18th-century prose writers what the heroic couplet did for the poets. Also, sentence/period boundaries have changed dramatically in literary English over the last 300 years, and our researchers felt that a code for analysis of added independent clauses would illuminate areas of that insistent shortening. Apart from word- and phrase-seriators (*and* = code 411), we now distinguish two other kinds of *and*. The first (code 416) adds a zeugmatic, elliptical, or minus-additioned independent clause, as in the examples below:

Jack and Jill went up the hill $\frac{416}{and}$ fetched a pail. . .

Father was worse, $\frac{416}{and}$ John much the same.

In short, 416 adds an independent clause from which anything (including the subject) has been omitted. Code 417 indicates an added clause as in the traditional compound sentence, a clause that could, as our school teachers taught us, "stand alone" if only punctuated differently. Code 417 does the following kinds of link:

Jack and Jill went up the hill $\frac{417}{and}$ they got into trouble.

John went East, $\frac{417}{and}$ Harry went West.

TABLE 1.3

York Inventory Word Classes

LEXEMES

01 NOUN
011 Noun
012 Attributive Noun
013 Possessive
014 Predicate Noun(1)
015 Noun/Subject(1)
016 Subj/Obj Complement(1)
017 Appositive(1)
018 Noun/Object
019 Noun/PrepPhr Completive

02 VERB
021 Active Verb
022 Passive Verb(1)
023 Ongoing Verb
024 Copula(1)

03 ADJECTIVE
031 Attributive Adjective
032 Predicate Adjective(1)
033 Participial Adjective
034 Subjective or Objective Complement
035 Postmodifying Adjective

04 ADVERB
041 Lexical Adverb

05 INFINITIVE
051 Active Infinitive
052 Passive Infinitive

06 PARTICIPLE
061 Active Participle
062 Passive Participle
068 Active Absolute
069 Passive Absolute

07 GERUND
071 Active Gerund
072 Passive Gerund

SPECIAL ITEMS
08 Miscellaneous Substantive, Foreignism
081 Misc. Substantive or Foreignism
082 Foreign quotation 8+ words

09 QUOTED MATERIAL
091 Quoted Word
092 Quotation 8+ words

FUNCTION WORDS
00 Ellipted rank-shift signal
001 Omitted Subordinator
002 Omitted Relative

11 PRONOUN
111 Prounoun
112 Reflexive
113 Negative
115 Subject
118 Object
119 PrePhr Completive

21 AUXILIARY + "BE"
211 Tense Aux (*Shall, will, have*)
212 Modal
213 *Be* finite predicator
214 *Be* auxiliary
215 *Be* infinitive
216 *Be* participle
217 *Be* gerund
218 *Be* absolute participle

31 DETERMINER
311 Definite Determiner
312 Possessive Pronoun
313 Indefinite Determiner

32 POSTPOSITION
321

33 INTENSIFIER
331

34 FUNCTION ADVERB
341 Possibility
342 Time
343 Place
344 Only
345 Qualifiction
346 *Never*

35 NEGATION
351 *No, Not, Nothing*

41 COORDINATOR
411 *And* for words & phrases
412 *But*
413 *For*
414 *Yet, As Well As, Rather Than*
415 *Or/Nor* for words & phrases

27

The data produced by our programs from the text parse involve word-classes, their distributions and their sequences. As I have indicated, however, other important distinctions are also possible, and it is useful to define just what is pointed to by the various terms with which those distinctions are made. We define some key-terms below.

Period/Sentence: We do not distinguish between these two: what is graphologically marked as a bound utterance we consider to be a sentence, i.e. terminally punctuated and followed by a capital letter at the beginning of the next word.

Clause: a structure containing (even by ellipsis) a predicator.

28

We classify clauses as follows:

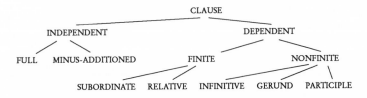

We have covered the two independent clauses. A *dependent clause* is marked for dependence by a class 42 or class 43 word, by a class oo ellipsis (the man oo2 I knew, we thought oo1 it was absurd), or by a *nonfinite* predicator. A nonfinite predicator is, by definition, *not ended*; i.e. it is unmarked by any of the suffixes that indicate aspect, mood, number, or person, though it *is* marked for tense and voice. The nonfinite verbs consist of what are sometimes called the verbals: infinitives, participles, and gerunds.

All the dependent clauses both finite (oo, 42, 43) and nonfinite (o5, o6, o7) are considered to be *rankshifted*. Since, in a theoretically hierarchical grammar that proceeds downward from Sentence to Clause to Phrase to Word, a clause should be a sentence component, any clause that functions as a component of a phrase or of another clause is functioning below its normal "rank" and is hence considered to be rankshifted. Rank-shifted clause totals per sample are an important index of complexity.

The most recent changes in our grammar, which enable us to tag clauses of *all* types and to make some important distinctions at the level of phrase structure, may seem inconsequential to the literary scholar with a belletristic or other non-linguistic orientation. But to the linguist, especially to the linguist interested in systemics, the descriptive improvements are all-important. To the linguist it is *essential* that a syntactic framework for the description of style be able to produce comprehensive information at all structural ranks (clause/phrase/word). It is important also that any style (that of a writer or that of a single text) be viewed against a background that includes the fullest possible information on time (temporal dialect), place (geographic dialect) and genre, so that generic, geographic, or temporal features of the text are not mistaken for things unique to the text or to its writer.

Parts of three of the four studies that follow in Part II have been previously published as prolusions. In one (chapter 6: Richler), the prolusion has survived nearly intact and constitutes roughly half of the text of the chapter: that original study was carried out within our current syntactic framework. In the other two (5 and 7: Davies and Atwood), the studies have been redone from the ground up in order to place the two writers properly against specifically Canadian norms and against specifically Canadian historical factors — as well as to put the findings into the most recent and most comprehensive syntactic model. In all three of these chapters, I have shifted the focus from the style of a *single* text (as it was in the prolusion) to the style of the writer.

The Ultimate Reward (Shapiro 11) of any critical act is an interpretive insight or two into the processes of a work or into the processes of the artist who produced it. In any of the non-language media, such insights are facilitated by the fact that the medium itself is exclusive in character, and its use is confined largely to artists or to those who aspire to be such. It is possible for ordinary people to live their entire adult lives without using paint or clay, or without conceiving or playing a single note of music. The case is, of course, different with a literary text, the roots of whose medium have long extensions into history and society, and indeed (like other art) into other works in the medium by way of allusion and generic convention. It was an attractive temptation to turn this book into a series of Ultimate Rewards — studies of individual works and writers, such as those in chapters 4 through 7.

It is an atavistic temptation, inviting one to become the child who comes to the dinner table only in order to eat the dessert. Interpretation is interesting, sometimes fascinating, work — certainly far more interesting than making decisions over whether an *and* is a 411, a 416, or a 417, over whether a preposition is a 511 or a 514. But humanistic scholarship had its beginnings in, and must ultimately rest upon, the work of what Samuel Johnson called harmless drudges: lexicographers, concordance-makers, and others who compile the stuff of the discipline. Good interpretation — i.e. interpretation truly arising from the text — must often be grounded in such stuff. It is primarily as a piece of *compilative* work that this book is put forward.

Contemporary scholarship often views the syntactic features of a text with lofty disdain (Watt). And though part of it is sometimes ignorance on the part of the critic, more often the problem lies in the simple dearth of information: nobody has compiled enough information about the syntactic practices of the literary community of a specific time and place. It is principally to such a deficiency that this book is addressed.

1. The alternative to printouts in the present system — tape — is more economical of space but requires access to a mainframe computer. Though colleagues in several other universities have used our data and programs (see *acknowledgments, supra*), the best access to the material for those who are not computer specialists remains the book.

2. The names most heard and seen are Jonathan Culler, Terry Eagleton, Michel Foucault, Jacques Derrida, Linda Hutcheon, Mary Nyquist, and Barbara Godard. Robert Scholes, much visible during the Barthes craze of a decade ago, seems (with Barthes) to have disappeared. This is a local survey (York).

3. Objective choice, by either random number table or random number generator, or by stratification (as the census does — every 4th, 6th or 10th house), is important. Unless the analysis is of a single continuous piece of substantial size (3,500 words) or is of objectively chosen cuts of the work, the results of the analysis are suspect — on the grounds that they might have been cooked.

4. Austen's *Prose Style* statistics (262–63) show her as highly predicative (more verbs than any other writer before Stein), sparing of adjectives and of word-parallelism (both of which often sources of overmanaged effects), rich in all the auxiliaries ("*must* be in search of a wife"), and highly pronominal.

5. *Cf.* Barbara Godard's recent excursion into the opening passage of *The Double Hook*, by Sheila Watson (" 'Between One Cliché and Another': Language in *The Double Hook*," in George Bowering, ed., *Sheila Watson and* The Double Hook [Ottawa: Oberon, 1985], 159 ff.). On a reading of Watson's whole book, one finds it difficult to accept the passage as any kind of typification.

6. Milic's original study (*A Quantitative Approach*) went to exhaustive lengths to prove this proposition with respect to Swift, whose style is generally conceded to have been fairly stable. *Prose Style* considers the case of Carlyle (178–215), who is rightly considered to have made major changes in his style between ages 25 and 30. Despite Carlyle's best efforts, there were remarkably stable elements between the *before* and *after* styles.

7. Ian Watt seems to express a view prevalent in the profession in his essay, "The First Paragraph of the Ambassadors: An Explication," when he indicates that stylistic inference "will lead one from the words on the page to matters as low as syntax and as high as ideas, or the total literary structure." A corollary to this notion is that literary study is about higher things, and therefore low things (like syntax) must perforce be ignored.

8. To be distinguished from the European tradition of Saussure, the structuralists, and the semioticists, and from the more recent American linguistics imported from Eastern Europe by Harris and Chomsky.

9. It is possible to accept the deconstructionists' "unstable text" as a figure of speech, a metonymy (the text as read, rather than the text itself). Adolph, on the other hand, seems to mean what he says quite literally.

10. See Halliday, *Language as Social Semiotic* 39: "I adopt the general perspective you find in Hjelmslev, in the Prague school, with Firth in the London school, with Lamb, and to a certain extent with Pike — language is a basically tristratal system: semantics, grammar, phonology. (Grammar means lexicogrammar; that is, it includes vocabulary.)"

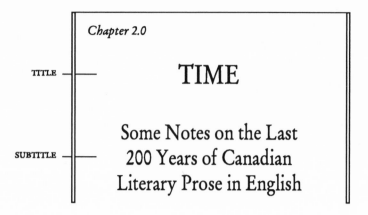

Chapter 2.0

TITLE

TIME

SUBTITLE

Some Notes on the Last
200 Years of Canadian
Literary Prose in English

HISTORY OF LANGUAGE / HISTORY OF STYLE

The history of the English *language* since 1500 has been, on the
syntactic side, one of glacial change, often imperceptible, from decade
to decade. On the other hand, the history of *prose style* in literary
English shows many changes, some rather sudden,[1] others more
gradual. It is the changes in prose style that this chapter will address.
The history of the *language* chronicles the general array of options
available or not available to the users of the language; the history of
style chronicles *which* of those options are actually chosen by writers
of the language over time. The language historian is likely to be
interested in facts like this: it is not possible, in 1990, for a speaker of
standard English to indicate a relative clause with the compound
particle *tha the*, as that particle went out in the Middle Ages. The
stylistic historian is likely to be interested in facts like this: "The man
I was speaking with" and "The man with whom I was speaking" are
both valid options in our own time, but the former is increasingly
preferred over the latter, to the point where the latter nowadays

sounds (especially in speech) either archaic or ostentatiously "correct."

A further important distinction for us to bear in mind is that when one speaks of the "history" of style, one speaks of a nugatory entity, an academic fiction. Though styles may clearly belong to periods, nobody writes wholly in *the style* of a given time in history; to do so, the writer would have to write at or near the mythical norm for the various formal features by which we might describe the period's writers, and nobody manages to do that, at least not in the real world.[2] The history of style, such as it is, is in fact the history of stylists — of how diverse and frequently divergent individuals make choices over time and of what (if any) the general drift of their preferences happens to be.

EVENTS IN GENERAL

Since the seventeenth century, several trends have characterized the world-wide development of expository nonfiction prose in English. One can delineate some of these trends by examining the history of, say, 15 word classes since 1600. In any large number of samples over the nearly 400 years, or even the latter half of this period, one will see increases in density of some classes, notably some classes of lexeme, and declines in the density of others, notably some classes of function word. Nouns, verbs, and modifiers (adjectives, adverbs, intensifiers, and function adverbs) increase over time, while the coordinators, subordinators, correlative conjunctions and sentence connectors all decline. These declines are both cause and effect of another trend: the distance in words from one terminal punctuation to the next — i.e. the length of bound utterance — is steadily shortened. All the forms of additioning are curbed: *copia verborum* increasingly is *OUT*; Hemingwayesque telegraphy increasingly is *IN*, so that one sees fewer and fewer compound sentences and a substantial decrease in all the other types of formal parallelism.[3] The sentence — indeed, the independent clause itself — gets less complex, as the density of rankshifted clauses declines, and there are major increases in the density of fragmentary sentences and of sentences with no finite dependent clauses in them. Use of the English language in Canada has partaken of these trends. We shall consider several of them as they develop over time, especially in Canada, doing so mainly under two heads: 1) *Reduction* in size and *simplification* of structure at sentence and clause level and 2) *DeFrancification* of all locutions, but especially of the noun phrase and the verb phrase. Let us consider these events as they are manifested in the 26 nonfiction samples of Table 1.1.

REDUCTION & SIMPLIFICATION

The most visible single long-term trend in modern English is the reduction in the size of the period. The trend is given dramatically visible form in Figure 2.1, reprinted from the 1976 York study. This trend is inseparable from one away from complexity and apparently just as inexorable. In the York Inventory the density of rankshifted clauses per sample shows a steady drop over time (Figure 2.2). These two things in conjunction with one another produce both a shorter and a simpler sentence, with shorter independent clauses and fewer rankshifted clauses per independent clause. Figures 2.3 and 2.4 show several parameters relating to two groups of samples from our Canadian selection. The groups are those writers born before 1830 and those born after 1912; the parameters are 1) rankshifted clauses per independent clause and its reciprocal (ICS per RSC), and 2) period length. The *before* and *after* pictures shown in 2.3 are given in textual form below, from Joseph Howe, writing in the early 1840s, and John Kenneth Galbraith, writing a century and a quarter later. Rankshifted clause markers have been italicized:

It is a mistake *to* suppose *that* genuine Eloquence is confined to the Pulpit, the forum, or the floors of Parliament. There are a thousand situations in *which* a good and brave man, by a few words well *chosen, spoken* with earnestness, and *deriving* weight from personal character, may serve himself, his neighbor, or his country. *Treating* of the most ordinary of these occasions, Bacon hath well said: "Discretion of speech is more than eloquence"; and "to speak agreeably to him with whom we deal, is more than to speak in good words or in good order."

Howe, *Poems and Essays* 226

The members of the technostructure do not get the profits *that* they maximize. They must eschew personal profit-making. Accordingly, *if* the traditional commitment to profit maximization is to be upheld, they must be willing to do for others, specifically the stockholders, *what* they are forbidden *to do* for themselves. It is on such grounds *that* the doctrine of maximization in the mature corporation now rests. It holds that the will *to* make profits is, like the will to sexual expression, a fundamental urge. But it holds *that* this urge operates not in the first person but in the third.

Galbraith, *New Industrial State* 128

The two passages are very nearly representative — the first, with a period length of 31.7 words and seven rankshifted clauses for three independent; the second, with a period length of 19.8 words and seven rankshifted clauses for six independent.

It is not just that the number of rankshifted clauses per sample diminishes with time (from a mean of 241 in our earliest six writers to a mean of 218 with our latest eight). Certain kinds of additioning of clauses fall gradually out of favour, specifically the compound sentence and the end-linking of relative clauses. The compound sentence — and indeed the general adding of all clauses including dependent ones — had its heyday in the 18th century. The 1982 York study showed an 18th-century mean of almost 60 coordinated clauses of all types per sample,[4] vs. a 20th-century mean of 37.2. The drop in compound sentences (i.e. in *and*-added and *or*-added independent clauses) was even more dramatic: from a mean of 46.2 to a mean of 21.4. As a percentage of all sentences, that latter drop is from 45.6% to 15.1%. In the present study, the first four Canadian figures showed a mean of 43.5 added independent clauses per 100 sentences; the remaining 22 showed a mean of barely a third that (14.66). Such a basic development needs no illustration beyond that provided in Figure 2.5 (Added Independent Clauses), but the related change, loss of end-linking, may need some in addition to Figures 2.6 (relatives) and 2.7 (431, non-restrictive relatives).

End-linking — extending a sentence by tacking a nonrestrictive relative clause on to what might otherwise have been a terminal noun — was a favourite syntactic device of the period 1600–1860. It particularly flourished through the 18th century, with Addison, Swift, Fielding, and Sterne all being constant users of the device. An example from Fielding:

Thus it happened to Nightingale, *who* no sooner found that Jones had no demand upon him, as he suspected, than he began to be pleased with his presence.

It is essentially a device of distribution — of moving emphasis from main to subordinate elements — and it remained widespread on into the 19th century, affected by writers as late as Herbert Spencer and Walter Pater, the latter of whom seems to have favoured any device that enabled him to go on . . . and on . . . and on. Dewart can illustrate his period's general affection for the terminal who/whom clause, both restrictive (433) and nonrestrictive (431):

It is not too much to say, that ordinary Christians *who* (433) hold the orthodox belief about the authorship of the books of the Bible have as good ground to be credited with independence as persons of similar learning *who* (433) accept the theories of the higher criticism on the authority of certain critics. The latter class accept theories *that* (433) are based on subtle distinctions and specu-lations, *whose* (431) import they but imperfectly understand.

Dewart, *The Bible under the Higher Criticism* 20

A similarly apt example of the terminal nonrestrictive comes from Bishop Strachan:

From the general view given, it would appear that the objects of the Society may be divided into two classes. The first relates to the immediate extension of the Church and the spiritual instruc-tion of our people, and seems to come more directly in its primary movement under the management of the clergy and churchwar-dens in their respective parishes, *whose* (431) business it will more particularly be to put the machinery into operation in their several congregations, as set forth in the rules and regulations of the Society.

Strachan, *Documents and Opinions*, 237

Note that the example also picks up the good Bishop's propensity for generating compound sentences. In keeping with his general practice (Figure 2.4), one sentence of two is compound. Let Berton show the practice of the present day, that of eschewing the relative clause option:

The attitude of the smug minority toward leisure is as confused as it is snobbish. Once again the terms have become muddied.

Hiram McCallum, Lord Beaverbrook, and *Industry* all speak of loafing. Neil McKinnon talks about laziness and James Duncan of indolence. None seems to believe that some of the time spent by some of the people away from their "work," *i.e.* the job, may be more creative than the time spent on the job; that it may, indeed, be of more value to the nation even though it is not included in the GNP.

Berton, *The Smug Minority* 57

The propositional content of the passage would lend itself readily to a style that resorted to relative clauses often (the smug minority, *who* ...; Neil McKinnon, *who* talks about laziness ...). But Berton does it his way — *our* way — and not the way of days gone by. In a further typification, in passages of the same length the Bishop gives us three coordinators where Berton gives us only two.[5]

Figure 2.9 gives coordinator numbers for each of the 26 writers in our group. The moderns use roughly two coordinators for every three used by the writers of the early 19th century.[6] Some of that reduction (and it is a *massive* reduction) comes from the decline of the compound sentence; the rest of it comes from the utilitarian stylistic ethic of the present day, which has rendered all seriation somewhat *outré*. Men and women, politicians and washroom attendants, students and scholars — all are taught to beware loquacity, together with its handmaidens "luxury and redundance of speech."[7] And with occasional exceptions like John Crosbie we are obedient to the teaching. Your three minutes are up. Please be brief. Figure 2.10 also shows the decline in word-parallelism. It is true that the device remains in 20th-century prose for serious use by scholars like Creighton and McLuhan and for devastating comic effects from novelists like Richler and Robert Coover. But the ethic of the time is strongly against it in non-comic, non-pedantic uses.

Francis Bacon, the fountainhead of utilitarianism in the English-speaking world and indeed the progenitor of the current stylistic ethic,[8] attacked those who valued *copia* over *weight*, and urged reform not only upon his English-speaking contemporaries but on all who would be his followers in later generations. 20th-century English has faithfully carried out his charge, in Canada no less than in other venues. Figure 2.11 shows what the stripping out of additive devices (removing coordinators) and what the systematic reduction of rank-shifted clauses (suppressing subordinators and relatives) have done to the historic proportion between the two large *phyla* of words in

English. In the 18th century, the function words were normally 60% of a text and the lexemes were 40%.[9] In 19th-century Canada the norm seems to have been 57–43. Figure 2.11 suggests that *normal* practice in present-day Canadian prose gives the function words less than 53%, the lexemes over 47% of text.

The Elements of Style, E.B. White's paean to the plain style ("Omit needless words!"), though an American book, has probably sold more copies in Canada than any other recent book on style.[10] Like most other hortatory volumes, it seems to have had little impact on practice. But its massive sale is an earnest of the fact that the sentiments of the literate public lie strongly with brevity and utility. Hence *weight* — the meaning words — steadily displaces connective tissue — the function words. A short look at D'Arcy McGee and Mordecai Richler will illustrate the shift (lexemes italicized):

> If we *take The Times* as a *sample* of our *daily press*, we will *find* that in the eighty *years* of its *existence* its *fortunes* have been *marked* by many *vicissitudes*. The first *Walter graduated* at *Newgate* for an *alleged libel* on the *sons* of *George III*, and is *said* to have *stood* in the *pillory*; while the second, some twenty *years ago*, *left* a *private fortune* to his *son*, in *city* and *country estates*, and a *personalty sworn* under £90,000 sterling.

McGee, Speeches and Addresses 37

> *Anti-heroes* and *heroines* may be *unconventionally handsome* or *beautiful*, but *handsome* and *beautiful* they still are. *Terence Stamp* and *David Hemmings*, who look *uncannily alike*, currently *filling* the *dubious office* of *hipsters' Andy Hardys*. Meanwhile *love*, except as *comic relief*, between a *short fat man* and a *flat-chested girl* is still beyond the *limits* of the *movies*.

Richler, Hunting Tigers Under Glass 99

The change is dramatic, with only 34 of the McGee passage's 80 items lexemes (42.5%); Richler, in a 54-word passage, gives us 28 (just over 50%). The contrast between the two is typical in other ways as well — McGee's density of rankshifted clauses, the differing lengths of period, the fragment in the Richler passage.

No writer, as we have noted, writes in the mythical average style of his time, except perhaps in a few parameters over a brief span, and it is impossible to discover two large samples, one of prose wholly typical of the early 19th century and another wholly typical of the mid-20th. It is, however, possible to offer, in Joseph Howe and John Diefenbaker, two glimpses of several of the trends we have thus far discussed working together: in period length, in seriation, and in end-linking.

We stand beside Niagara, or beneath the dome of St. Peter's, or St. Paul's, and are overpowered by a sense of sublimity and beauty, for which we thank God, but which it is extremely difficult to analyze. We hang over a beautiful statute [*sic*], or gaze at a fine picture, but are lost and bewildered when we come to describe why it touches our feelings, or excites our involuntary admiration.

Howe, Poems and Essays 208

I encountered an unexpected problem on my arrival in Wakaw. I knew, of course, that I was breaking in on a lawyer who had set up practice the year before. I had, however, known him in law school and I knew that he was not particularly interested in litigation. What I did not know was that many of Wakaw's leading businessmen, out of friendship for him, were determined to shut me out if they could. I found, for example, that I was not too welcome at the local hotel, which provided the town's only decent accommodation. I was forced to spend my first two months in a rented room about seven feet by eight, a near approach to an enlarged piano box.

Diefenbaker, One Canada 57

DEFRANCIFICATION

Not all of the historical shift towards the lexemes is accounted for by changes in sentence- and clause-architecture. Much of it, in fact, arises from alteration of phrase-structure. This, too, undergoes an *apparent* reduction and simplification and may well indicate that nearly half a millenium after the Renaissance humanists imposed Latinesque and Francophonic locutions upon our barbarous Nordic tongue — housebreaking the Hun, pomading his hair, and stuffing him into the straitjacket of a Paris suit — the essentially Germanic character of the

39

English language is reasserting itself. This process, the Germanic revival, might have been set in motion by David Hume with his trend-setting public visit to Germany in 1764; what had long been *verboten* suddenly became *au courant*. Linguistically, the founder and hero — quite consciously the hero — of the movement was undeniably Thomas Carlyle (*Prose Style*). Whether one calls the trend a Germanic revival, or a regression, or a barbarization[11] matters not: the name that best seems to fit the facts is DeFrancification, as it suggests the most probable general event represented by the particular choices writers made with respect to phrase structure as time went on. It all amounted to the gradual removal of much of the French overlay that was imposed on the syntax of the language by the Renaissance humanists and their heirs between 1500 and 1700.[12]

Figure 2.12 shows auxiliaries as a percentage of finite verb phrase heads. Even though the language has grown more predicative over time, with more finite clauses for a given body of text, the density of auxiliary verbs has declined. The figure shows a decline since the early 19th century from .536 auxiliaries per finite verb phrase to .426.[13] That is a 20% decline — a major event that takes place despite the increase in verb phrases of ongoing aspect, each of which requires at least one auxiliary (Figure 2.13). One component of that decline is a loss of present-perfect and past-perfect constructions — from roughly 18% of all verb phrases to 14%. Bishop Strachan, as always, can furnish an excellent 19th-century benchmark (auxiliaries, Class 21, underlined):

Dearly beloved in the Lord,
The clergy and lay members of the Church, moved by a pious desire to promote the glory of God, and the welfare of the flock of his diocese, over which, however unworthy, he *hath* made me Overseer, *have* represented unto me that the Church *is* suffering from the want of greater unity of action: that her future progress *will be* much impeded unless steps *are* speedily taken to provide for her growing strength and efficiency as the population increases . . . .

Strachan, *Documents and Opinions* 236

Richler can represent the 20th century, in exaggerated form, not only for loss of verb auxiliaries, especially loss of the perfective *have*, but also for the growth of two germanic forms represented in Figures 2.13 and 2.14 — the ongoing aspect verb phrase (be + *ing* — head coded 023) and the postposition verb (02 + 321: *get up, buzz off, look out*).

Renaissance humanism and its inheritors taught us always to prefer the Latin or Romance form to the Germanic form — to *arise* rather than *get up*, to *initiate* rather than *start up*, to *depart* rather than *take off*. Richler gives earnest that we are unlearning those lessons rapidly (auxiliaries italicized, ongoing aspect heads marked 023, postpositions marked 321):

> Mailer began by promising us a definition of existentialism, which he never quite got around (321) to. He spoke with regret for the eighteenth century when society was orderly and the British navy and the orgasm *were* both going (023) good; and then he remembered to put in (321) a word for the folks in Alaska who live in a heroic relation to nature.
>
> Richler, *Hunting Tigers Under Glass* 105

Farther on in the same passage, we have Mailer "going *on* and *on*" plus "let *down*" and an irregular tricolon of ongoing-aspect verbs: "nearly everybody was making (023) condescending jokes, shaking (023) their heads, and feeling (023) sorry for Mailer" (Figure 2.14).

Parallel with the decline of the perfective tenses is a decline of the infinitive — again something approaching 20% between the early 19th century and the middle of the 20th (Figure 2.15). Though the infinitive exists in both French and German, the French seem to affect its use far more than their northern neighbours do. Thus the loss of infinitives would seem to be a part of the DeFrancification process. Joseph Howe, soaring into an infinite empyrean, could declare:

> I say a firm conviction, because men may accept truth, without feeling its value very intensely, and such will ever lack the inspiration *to proclaim* it — *to suffer* — *to die* for it.
>
> Howe, *Poems and Essays* 236

And Peter C. Newman, speaking in a style that, for our day, is no less grand than Howe's was for his:

> By early spring, Diefenbaker was acting as if he were contriving ruin with a finality his most dedicated enemies could hardly have hoped *to achieve*. Faced by the desertion of all but the tightening inner circle of his one-time followers, John Diefenbaker now was concerned only with the rude chance of his own political survival. A man of lacerated ego and exhausted sensibilities, famished for popularity and denied understanding, he turned himself into a

kind of ideological nomad in his own land, romanticizing the soaring windmills in the blazing frescoes of his imagination. He retreated into the world of his own which he roamed vainly searching for the elusive touchstones of power.

Newman, *A Nation Divided* 153

The incidence of a single infinitive in a passage of roughly 130 words (24 per sample) is only half of the 20th-century mean, but the choice of participle clauses in preference to serial infinitives typifies the difference between our time and Howe's.

Part of the historical process of the growth of the lexemes' share of text has been increasing nominalization: the density of nouns will usually be far greater in a 20th-century text than in an 18th-century text. The difference between our own time and the 19th century is somewhat less, but it is still there and is consequential. The 1982 York study indicated that most nouns in literary English prior to 1900 had some kind of prepositional connexion,[14] with 51% of all nouns in literary prose to that date serving as completives in prepositional phrases, and an additional indeterminate percentage (5–14%) serving as heads of noun phrases qualified by a prepositional phrase.

In theory, then, if the language frame were to stay stable as between positively related items,[15] an increase in nouns should bring with it an increase in prepositions. Figure 2.16 shows that this did not in fact happen among our Canadians.[16] As the nominals were registering roughly a 5% gain between the coronation of Victoria and that of Trudeau, the prepositions were registering a 10% decline. The ratio of preposition to noun goes from roughly 10:17 to 10:20, or from 59% down to 50%. The principal instrument of that decline is the increasing use of the attributive noun, which is usually a transformed prepositional phrase; under that transformation, Francophonic *top of the table* becomes germanic *table top*, *builder of homes* becomes *home builder*, and *oil for the lubricating of aircraft* becomes *aircraft lubrication petroleum products*. Even the most obtuse Frenchman can see that attributive noun use is, in Arte Johnson's phrase, *more efficienter* than attempts at tuning one's instrument to the melodic key of the Francophones: put aside your morning paper some day and take ten minutes to consider the English and the French on your bran flakes box. Figure 2.17 (attributive nouns) accounts for roughly half the loss of prepositions shown in Figure 2.16; the remaining half arises in part from something similar — increasing use of possessives[17] — and in part from a decline (roughly 20 per sample) in the adverbial use of prepositional phrases. At the same time, as the place to the right of the noun gets vacated by the prepositional phrase, we are more inclined than before (Figure 2.18) to use apposition. It is interesting in this connexion that our selection's most prolific attributive generator is also most prolific in appositives: Richler.

In most of our studies, the "M" statistic (numerical total of all modifiers — adjective, adverb, intensifier, function adverb) for the 20th century is higher than that for the early 19th. The range of increase in the various studies has been between 7% and 10%. In the Canadian group, the increase is 9.2% (Figure 2.19). Again, in most of our studies, the components of that group most likely to increase are the adjectives, the function adverbs and the intensifiers. This indeed is what happens in Canada between Joseph Howe and Robert Fulford or between D'Arcy McGee and Donald Creighton. Why it happens is a mystery in some ways, though it is certainly possible to relate the increase in adjective use to the rise in the number of nouns. My own habit of mind is to associate the modifying words with soap opera and advertising — doubtless a prejudiced judgement but one that is reinforced by the fact that among our Canadian fiction writers the only two to produce "M" statistics that reach 500 were Mazo de la Roche and Lucy Maude Montgomery. A trial sample of a Harlequin Romance yielded an "M" of 587. A final observation on Figure 2.19 is that the poets and novelists in the group (Atwood, Layton, Callaghan, Davies, and Richler) are pretty ruthless editors of their own stuff. No Madison Avenue, Young and Restless, Young and Rubicam, heartrending torrents of modification for them. The academics, on the other hand . . .

The trends discussed in this chapter are not happening in isolation. Table 2.1 shows comparisons of the Canadian data with data from previous studies and with data from a 40-author Anglo-American control group. The trends visible in Canada are visible also in Great Britain and the U.S.A.[18] The only two shifts visible in the Canadian writers not confirmed by the Anglo-American control sample are the shifts in coordinators and in word-parallelism, and these shifts have already been indicated by the larger samplings of both the 1976 and 1982 York studies. A look at Appendix A will show the reason for the peculiarity of the present control group: Jefferson, Cooper, and Huxley are distinctly sparing of additive devices for their time; Joyce and Stein are uniquely copious adders for theirs.

The discovery that changes in the stylistic preferences of Canadian writers in English parallel those of their British and American colleagues is an important one, since it suggests that if there is a specific linguistic place called Canada, its boundaries may be defined by phonology, subject matter, and lexis rather than by syntax. Of this question, more in chapter 8.

CONCLUSIONS

We are clearly moving in the direction of Bauhaus language: more and more is being left out, so that less is more. In drama and poetry the 20th century has produced numerous theorists and practitioners who speak forcefully for some kind of minimal aesthetic of language: Stein, Hemingway, Callaghan, Beckett, W.C. Williams, Robert Creeley, Eli Mandel, and Margaret Atwood to name only a few. What is happening in expository prose is different; it has different sources and different reasons. Its reasons have to do with utility rather than aesthetics, and its sources are not artists. Its sources are philosophers, teachers, and practitioners, most popularly in our own day Will Strunk, E.B. White, and Rudolph Flesch.

The utilitarian aesthetic has been the dominant one in English prose style for three and a quarter centuries, its acceptance as the consensus view coinciding with the founding of the Royal Society in 1661 (Adolph). Those who write a more expansive style of prose for aesthetic reasons (Henry James, Frederick Buechner, Robertson Davies)[19] and those who affect linguistic archaism for political reasons (William F. Buckley, Robertson Davies, Harold Nicolson) are out of step with the direction of progress, more often than not consciously so. Few, indeed very few nowadays, would undertake to defend euphemism, periphrasis, indirection, or any other habit that results in circuit of speech or taking the long way round. These are, after all, not in accord with the *zeitgeist*, being as they are devices associated with good manners and civilized speech. And, in William of Wyckeham's motto, "Manners makyth Man."[20] But in our age it is with Osric rather than with William of Wyckeham that non-utilitarian devices are associated: Francophonic phrasing has become the lace cuff of literary fashion, sneered at as "degenerate and effeminacious"[21]

44

by those who like their meat red, their tenses simple, and their nouns arrayed in efficient orderly freight train phrases.

Barbarization and germanicizing have fallen under attack lately from various sources. Thirty years ago, Edmund Fuller wrote an extended Philippic denouncing the model of humanity accepted by the writers of mid-century, a model specifically derived from and much reinforced by the work of the social sciences (i.e. the German academic disciplines), which also happen to be the most egregious progenitors and propogators of aneurism-style, blood-clot *allgemeinenounenlumpen*: "aggression-hostility syndrome" or "infant care deprivation side effects." More recently George Steiner has attacked certain Germanic elements in our vocabulary, notably the tetragrams,[22] and several contemporary rhetoricians have bemoaned the antisocial, antihistorical tendencies both of contemporary criticism and of contemporary language itself — notably Wayne Booth, Gerald Graff, and Allan Bloom.

By far the most deeply felt and most coherently thought out attack on the germanicizing of the English-speaking world has come in a novel — from Philip Roth in *Portnoy's Complaint*. Many things are attacked in the book, laughed at, even savaged. Four of these things — and Roth clearly sees them as related to one another — are focal: contemporary sexual mores, contemporary trends in language (especially as regards use of the formerly taboo Germanic tetragrams), psychoanalysis in the Viennese mode, and the loss of dialogue that characterizes all three of these. The malady "Portnoy's Complaint" is mockingly defined in the book's introduction as a psychological syndrome in which humanitarian impulses war with the basest, vilest, most degrading sexual urges; the definition is something of a red herring, for the complaint here is like "The Complaint of Rosamund": a love-object has been lost, in this case Alex Portnoy's penis. On a pilgrimage to Israel, Alex is afflicted with impotence, for which he puts himself into analysis with the aptly named Doctor Spielvogel (literally, "Doctor Masturbation," the German roots of whose name are the verb *spielen*, to play, and the noun *Vogel*, bird: Freudian analysis amounts to playing with your bird). The book is a putative transcription of Alex's outpourings to the doctor. In its time, it probably set a new high-water mark for density of tetragrams in a trade book, and it certainly pushed back a few frontiers in trade publishing with regard to sexual practices: Alex, in addition to being a highly innovative masturbator, a total male chauvinist (before that term was even invented), and an egotist of titanic proportions, is —

until his bout with misfortune in the old country — an insatiable practitioner of *cunnilingus*. Alex's phony, Mayor Lindsay style humanitarianism, his strictly instrumental vision of language, his instrumental view of the opposite sex, his belief in the possible efficacy of a Viennese cure for his impotence, and indeed the impotence itself are all of a piece. Alex, the supreme utilitarian, discovers himself unable even to find (much less grasp) beauty, creativity, decency, goodness, or power. Though he clearly longs for them, he lacks the requisite tools for their having. Indecorous Alex, having spent so much time with his head where his penis should be, becomes *literally* impotent, and his language — like his love life — so rich in those germanic derivatives, in the end is nothing but oral sex. Not real sex, oral sex: talk. "What does Portnoy have to do with Canada?" you say, "The locus of all those things is Manhattan, miles and miles from Toronto the Good, even farther from Edmonton." Yes, it is true that Alex's style is the style not only of his time but of his place. But Roth's vision is the one that has come closest to seeing the problem whole, and it *is* our problem, for the language events in other English-speaking cultures become our language events, too. Edmund Fuller's dehumanized humanity, George Steiner's despised four-letter words, the Germanic detestation of absolute value attacked by Bloom, and the loss of civilized dialogue bemoaned by Booth and Graff all in some degree afflict us, and they do so not separately but as a *gestalt*. Developments in syntax are part of that *gestalt*. Defeating the Hun was easy when it had to be done only at the conscious level — as in World War I and World War II. At the unconscious level it has proven more difficult, perhaps impossible, because more and more we speak his language.

Stylistic utilitarianism is as pervasive in English Canada as it is in the U.S.A. or the U.K. It will no doubt continue to thrive: there are manuals to be written, instructions to be given, and things to be communicated throughout the worlds of business, science, politics, and technology. Whether or not it *should* continue to thrive in the literary context is moot. It has undeniably helped to produce a language that gets things done, that does its work efficiently. But the little bitty bare-ass version of English[23] in vogue today may fail to convey nuance with the clarity or self-assurance, say, of the language of Henry James. What it does do very well indeed is perhaps best epitomized by President Reagan's inadvertent radio address during the 1984 American election campaign: "The bombs start dropping in five minutes." Useful, direct, efficient: lexemes 4, function words 3.

1. See *Prose Style*, chapter 9. Most changes are gradual, though there is the occasional sudden one, such as the loss of initial connexion of sentences among secular writers at the beginning of the 18th century.

2. Besides the impossibility of anybody's being completely average, the stylistic historian faces the truculent and ambiguous fact that at any point in history there are many different temporal states of the language coexisting. Thomas Carlyle and Nathanael West live on trend-lines that are 50-100 years into the future from the times in which they wrote. Bishop George Berkeley, Cardinal John Henry Newman, and Professor Robertson Davies all have written in styles deliberately archaic.

3. In the 1976 York study, six of 13 19th-century writers had over 100 word-parallelisms in their samples, only two of 12 in the 20th (Scott Fitzgerald and Lewis Mumford). The means for the two centuries were, respectively 98.9 and 88.4, both figures down substantially from the 17th-century mean of 106.7.

4. The 1982 York study considered 50 writers from Ascham to 1975 and did so under an experimental coding system of which the present system is modification. The samples were considered only for subcategories under 01 (Noun), 11 (Pronoun), 41 (Coordinator), 43 (Relative), and 51 (Preposition). We kept four of the sets of subcategories, re-modifying the coordinator subcategories because the 1982 model did not distinguish between a minus-added independent clause and a minus-added dependent clause. There being only 10 slots between 411 and 410, we always have a problem with how to cut up the coordinator system.

5. Note also that Berton has only one (minus-additioned) compounded clause in four sentences, five independent clauses.

6. The loss of coordinators between the early 19th and mid-20th centuries is confirmed by nearly every study we have made. In the 1976 York study the mean (1800–40) was 174.2, with a mean (1930–75) of 145.1 (Figure 2.8); in the 1982 study, the comparable figures were 168.5 and 141.4. The loss is more severe in our Canadian selection, but the direction of the trend is the same.

7. In one of the most famous passages in the history of prose style, Thomas Sprat (112) fastened this phrase on to all non-utilitarian styles.

8. For the full account, see Robert Adolph, *The Rise of Modern Prose Style*.

9. See Milic; see also *Prose Style*, chapter 9.

10. The publisher, Macmillan, does not release separate figures for Canadian sales, but offers the offhand estimate of "200,000 to 225,000 copies for Canada alone."

11. George Steiner, in his essay "Literature and Post-History," identifies numerous Germanic leitmotivs in present-day culture and elsewhere has repeatedly inveighed against the four-letter words as an element in the barbarization of our language. Nowhere, to my knowledge, has he specifically related the two to each other.

12. In the boarding school to which my parents dispatched me not long after my 13th birthday, a hands-to-work, hearts-to-God parody of the great humanist-founded schools of England such as Winchester and Eton, it was not uncommon for one to be threatened with corporal punishment for use of an attributive noun

(Germanic) where it was possible to use a prepositional phrase (Francophonic). If one persisted in Germanic noun phrase construction habits, one occasionally did get, in the best tradition of the English schools, a savage caning.

13. The decline is similar in our Anglo-American control samples. For a full comparison, see table 2.1 at the end of the chapter.

14. In that 1982 study, 51% of all nouns were completives (Class 019). In addition, a number of prepositions amounting to 29.5% of all nouns were heads of noun-modifying prepositional phrases (Class 514). One cannot simply add Class 019 and Class 514 to arrive at a percentage of prepositionally related nouns, because there is overlap between the two classes: for example, the phrase *at the home of my father* contains two nouns class 019 and one preposition class 514 (of).

15. In the 1976 study, we found the four highest correlations among the various word classes to be as follows (Pearson's *r*): preposition-determiner (.68), preposition-adjective (.46), adjective-noun (.39), and preposition-noun (.36) (*Prose Style* 274).

16. Note from the figure that as the *number* of nouns increases, the *number* of prepositions decreases.

17. From a mean of 6.2 in our early group to a mean of 15.1.

18. We have no data on Australia and New Zealand, but our hunch is that they would reflect nearly all of the same trends.

19. For a fuller exploration of Davies's linguistic conservatism, see chapter 5, below.

20. Motto of Winchester College, founded by William of Wyckeham in 1383 in Winchester, Hants. It is England's premier "public" school.

21. Thomas Browne, *Vulgar Errors*, "The Hare."

22. Most critics favour the term "four-letter word." I do not. My preference is for the more oblique *tetragram*; the English version is *too* direct, and conjures up thoughts of the words themselves. *Vide* Steiner, in "Eros and Idiom" from *George Steiner: A Reader:* "In the 'new freedom' there is more than a touch of bullying. Our imaginings are programmed, obscene words are shouted at the inner ear. The new idiom has made it difficult to distinguish between integrity and mendacity . . . The present code of sexual explicitness may be related to the general *malaise* of the novel. The inhumanities of speech and action so obsessively reproduced in many important contemporary novels have, as their natural counterpart, the 'non-humanity' of the *nouveau roman*" (343).

23. There is a double allusion in this phrase. In *Across the River and into the Trees*, Colonel Cantwell, recalling one of his many acts of military bravery, narrates an account of how his men tackled "a little bitty bare-ass hillside." E.B. White, in a parody of the book, picked up the phrase as "a little bitty bare-ass highboy."

48

TABLE 2.1

Comparison Figures: 1800-1840 vs. 1930-1975, Three Studies

			1987 CAN LIT (This book)	1987 ANGLO-AM (This Book)	1982 YORK	1976 YORK (PS&CR)
Fig 2.3	19C	RSC:IC	1.31	1.47	N.A.	N.A.
	20C	RSC:IC	.96	.98	N.A.	N.A.
Fig 2.3	19C	IC:RSC	.76	.69	N.A.	N.A.
	20C	IC:RSC	1.05	1.02	N.A.	N.A.
Fig 2.4	19C	P.L.	33.3	33.2	N.A.	33.3
	20C	P.L.	22.6	24.4	N.A.	27.3
Fig 2.5	19C	+ICS(%)	39.5	38.1	45.6	N.A.
	20C	+ICS(%)	14.6	19.7	25.1	N.A.
Fig 2.6	19C	43 total	52.0	56.5	61.9	58.2
	20C	43 total	45.6	47.0	51.2	45.6
Fig 2.7	19C	43NRRC	20.3	N.A.	23.9	24.1
	20C	43NRRC	11.7	N.A.	15.8	12.6
Fig 2.9	19C	41	173.6	[141.6] 1	168.5	174.2
	20C	41	134.8	[164.6]	141.4	145.1
Fig 2.10	19C	//ism	111.2	[67.2] 2	106.1	114.7
	20C	//ism	92.2	[81.5]	88.7	93.5
Fig 2.11	19C	Lexemes	43.0	41.6	N.A.	43.0
	20C	Lexemes	46.7	43.6	N.A.	46.2
Fig 2.12	19C	Aux/Pred	.536	.574	N.A.	N.A.
	20C	Aux/Pred	.426	.402	N.A.	N.A.
Fig 2.14	19C	023	5.7	3.6	N.A.	6.1
	20C	023	10.6	7.2	N.A.	10.3
Fig 2.13	19C	321	14.7	12.7	N.A.	N.A.
	20C	321	19.9	19.4	N.A.	N.A.
Fig 2.15	19C	05(Inf Cl)	58.0	61.2	N.A.	46.2
	20C	05(Inf Cl)	48.8	43.5	N.A.	39.9
Fig 2.16	19C	51:01	58.8	65.4	N.A.	62.3
	20C	51:01	50.2	52.6	N.A.	51.8
Fig 2.17	19C	012	8.5	20.4	N.A.	23.6
	20C	012	36.2	37.6	N.A.	48.8
Fig 2.18	19C	017	14.2	7.2	N.A.	N.A.
	20C	017	23.5	20.3	N.A.	N.A.
Fig 2.19	19C	M	407.6	440.8	N.A.	[521.2] 3
	20C	M	443.1	457.4	N.A.	[455.8]

N.A. means not available: the parameters involved in the Figure were not part of that study. The three bracketed sets of numbers are sports, the 19c-20c trend for the parameter involved in each case being a contrary instance. Except for class 41 (1), the 20th century figures agree with those in the other studies. In all three cases, it is mainly the 19th century figures that are incompatible — principally, I suspect, because of the small number of writers in the sample (five for 1987, three for 1976), together with the presence of writers who are massively deviant in one parameter or another: Jefferson, Cooper and Huxley among the 1987 Anglo-Americans; Carlyle among the 1976 Victorians. One screwball will not disrupt a study covering eight or more writers, but may severely disturb a study covering five (1987) or three (1976).

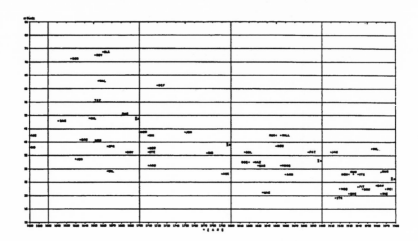

FIGURE 2.1
Period Length

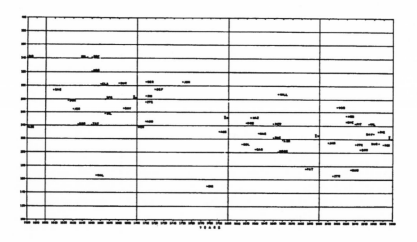

FIGURE 2.2
Rank Shifting

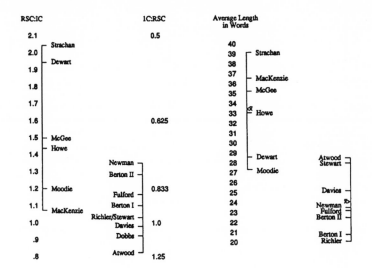

FIGURE 2.3
Rankshifted Clauses (RSC),
Independent Clauses (IC): Ratios

FIGURE 2.4
Period Length

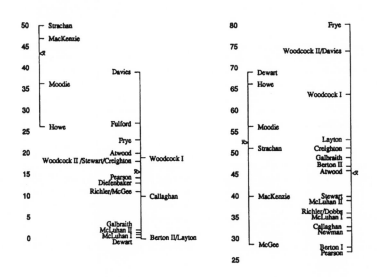

FIGURE 2.5
And/or — Added Independent
Clauses as % of Total Periods

FIGURE 2.6
Relatives (43)

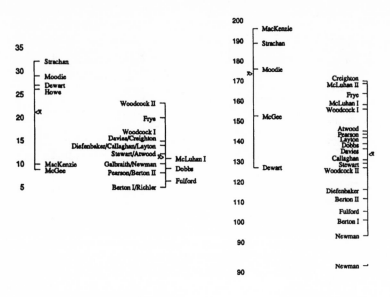

35	200 ⌐ MacKenzie
	190 ⌐ Strachan
30 ⌐ Strachan	180
⌐ Moodie	⌐ Moodie
⌐ Dewart	170
25 ⌐ Howe	
	160 Creighton McLuhan II
⌐ Woodcock II	Frye
20 α	150 ⌐ McGee
⌐ Frye	

(chart labels)

FIGURE 2.7

Nonrestrictive Relatives (431)

FIGURE 2.9

Coordinators (41)

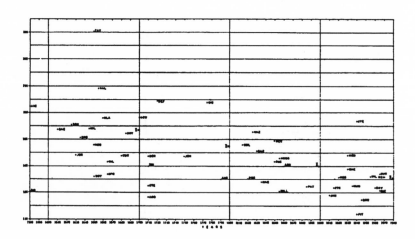

FIGURE 2.8

Coordinators (Class 41)

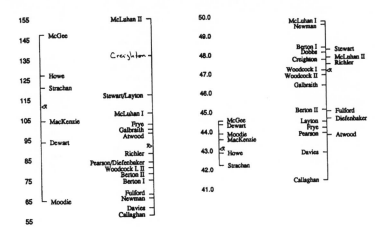

FIGURE 2.IO

Word Parallelism

FIGURE 2.II

Lexemes as % of Text

(01 + 02 + 03 + 04 + 05 + 06 + 07)

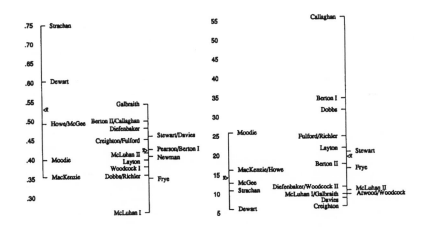

FIGURE 2.12

Auxiliaries as % of all Finite Verb
Phrases (21-213/02 + 213)

FIGURE 2.I3

Postpositions (32)

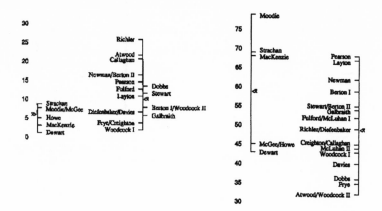

FIGURE 2.14

Ongoing Aspect Verbs (023)

FIGURE 2.15

Infinitive Clauses (05)

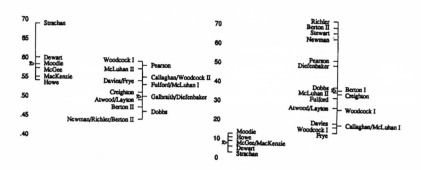

FIGURE 2.16

Preposition : Noun Ratio (51 : 01)

FIGURE 2.17

Attributive Nouns (012)

54

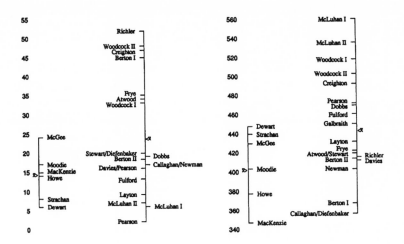

FIGURE 2.18

Appositive Nouns (017)

FIGURE 2.19

"M" Statistic

(03 + 04 + 33 + 34)

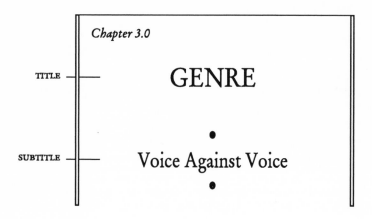

Chapter 3.0

TITLE

GENRE

•

SUBTITLE

Voice Against Voice

•

Our thinking about genres tends to focus on the relationship between artist and material (is the account "true" or fabricated?),[1] sometimes on certain formulaic devices, as in the *aubade* or the sonnet (Nelson 87–117). Where language comes under scrutiny as an aspect of genre, it is either lexis (Colie 3–9; Hunter 71), or the kinds of figures employed (Strelka 5–8), or the functional tenor (e.g. — mode of address) (Strelka 138) that is likely to catch the scholarly eye. Syntax as an aspect of genre has not received widespread attention — difficult though it may be to have a comprehensive discussion of either an heroic couplet or a sonnet without some attention being given to sentence layout and clausal ordering. With the exception of some of Barron Brainerd's studies of word-class incidence, literary scholarship in its studies of genre has tended to show the same diffidence about syntactic matters that it has shown elsewhere. In this case, there may be grounds: few of us would not be diffident about performing lengthy empirical studies to demonstrate that "I" occurs more frequently in autobiography than in other genres: for though the rediscovery of the obvious may be the principal product of literary scholarship, the scholarly community expects such rediscovery to be done with "style" (in Jakobsen's sense), and it is difficult indeed to be stylish about the autobiography and "I." In summoning the muse, therefore, for the chapter that follows, I have bid her make a particular effort that my labours be attended with stylishness, and that they not just be driven by what is, inevitably, my style.

"Genre" for our purposes here is not a highly restricted concept: it is narrative and descriptive and expository prose divided simply as fiction and nonfiction, the dividing question being one of personeity: Is this the real Margaret Atwood or Anthony Burgess or Robertson Davies speaking or is it a *persona* — omniscient narrator or character in a novel? For logistical and other reasons, we have excluded all dialogue from both kinds of sample, setting dialogue aside as a matter to return to later. If one were to do otherwise, the confusions generated by sentence- and utterance-boundaries would be substantial, and this is only the first and most visible difficulty arising from samples that mix dialogue (usually written to be read as if overheard) with narration and description (usually written to be read, or, if written in a speaking voice, written to be read as if heard).

Within our 53 Canadian samples and within the 40 Anglo-American control samples, there are major quantitative differences between nonfiction and fiction. They suggest that genre does indeed have a substantial influence on syntax: taken all together, the fiction samples have shorter clauses, have fewer rankshifted clauses, are more predicative, and are both more pronominal and less nominal than the nonfiction samples. However, in both the total Canadian group and the total Anglo-American group, the writers on the nonfiction side are not always the same people as those on the fiction side, so that the comparison of genres using all the writers may be impaired by the influence of author-style. I have therefore confined the close scrutiny of text-with-numbers in this chapter to eight writers that are represented in both the nonfiction and the fiction group. The eight writers, together with their sixteen samples, are listed in Table 3.1.

TABLE 3.1

British & Canadian Writers: Nonfiction & Fiction

BRITISH WRITERS	NONFICTION	FICTION
E.M. Forster	Aspects of the Novel	Passage to India
Virginia Woolf	The Common Reader (I)	To the Lighthouse
George Orwell	Essays	1984
Anthony Burgess	The Novel Now	MF

CANADIAN WRITERS	NONFICTION	FICTION
Morley Callaghan	That Summer in Paris	A Native Argosy/ Strange Fugitive
Robertson Davies	A Voice from the Attic	Fifth Business
Mordecai Richler	Hunting Tigers...	Duddy Kravitz
Margaret Atwood	Survival	The Edible Woman

Many measures tended to show substantial change between nonfiction and fiction. None of these measures is an infallible indicator of genre. For example — though we cannot derive genre from a number (e.g. "5 uses of *I* every 100 words makes an autobiography"), it is evident that fiction tends to bend style in some very clear directions. We shall consider those directions under three headings: sentences and compounding, predication and clausal arrays, and word-classes and word-class groups.

SENTENCES AND COMPOUNDING

Fiction begets tidiness in prose. Forget Cozzens, Wouk, and Michener with their nine-pound turgid tomes: the verdict of this selection of writers — both the eight writers focussed on in this chapter and the 72 others in our 93 samples — is that the act of realizing something imaginatively produces cleaner, less cluttered writing than does trying to realize something propositionally.[2] The most immediately visible area of this tidiness is the way sentences are put together. When a writer moves from nonfiction to fiction, the average length of an independent clause shows a marked decrease—in both the British and the Canadian group. Among the Brits the average independent clause drops from 14.8 to 12.9 words, among the Canadians, the independent clause drops from a mean of 14.0 to a mean of 11.1 words. This produces a major increase from genre to genre in the total number of independent clauses per sample (Figure 3.1): it occurs in every single one of our eight writers. Together with it (this time in only six of the eight, but still to the extent of about 5% of the means), there is a visible but less marked drop in the number of rankshifted clauses (Figure 3.2). These two movements combined drop the mean ratio of rank-shifted clauses to independent clauses from 1:1 to .85:1 among the Brits and to .79:1 among the four Canadians. The change in this ratio is visible in seven of the eight writers (Figure 3.3), and it suggests that one of the strong generic "pulls" of the novel is towards a less hypotactic, more paratactic style. Richler can illustrate (rank-shift markers italicized):

> Nine storeys high with an enormous lobby, a sweep of red-carpeted stairway, and endless corridors *leading* here, there, and everywhere, the Concord can cope with 2,500 guests *who* can I'm assured, consume 9,000 latkas and ten tons of meat a day. Ornate chandeliers drip from the ceiling of the main lobby. The largest of the hotel's three nightclubs, the Imperial Room, seats 2,500 people. But it is dangerous *to attempt* a physical description of the hotel. For even *as* I checked in, the main diningroom was making way for a still larger one, and it is just possible *that since* I left, the five inter-connecting convention halls have been opened up and converted into an indoor spring training camp for the Mets. Nothing's impossible.
>
> Richler, *Hunting Tigers* 138

The ratio of seven rankshifted clauses for seven independent is exactly on the mean. Consider Richler in fiction, dealing with other entertainments in another summer resort:

> The lights in the recreation hall were turned out and the front door was locked. Fifteen minutes later some of the lights were turned on again and a side door was opened. The players began *to arrive.* Duddy set up the table and announced the odds in a failing voice. He would pay thirty to one on a full number and

the top bet *allowed* was fifty cents. That would pay fifteen dollars, one-fifty of *which* would go into the JNF box. Linda, *who* was helping him, began *to sell* change. Farber bought five dollars worth and Mr. Cohen asked for ten. *Once* Duddy had counted forty players in the hall he asked for the door *to be shut*.

Richler, Duddy Kravitz 86

The comparison exaggerates somewhat — but only somewhat — the differences between the Richler samples shown in Figures 3.1, 3.2, and 3.3. In passages of similar length above, the number of independent clauses doubles (from 7 to 14) and the number of rankshifted clauses stays the same (7). Notice also the four compound sentences in the second passage, in comparison with only one in the first.

This gets us to a second aspect of the paratactic "pull" of fiction — and again a strongly visible one: the density of *and-* and *or-* added independent clauses, with increases ranging from 12% on up into the hundreds.[3] Figure 3.4 shows our eight writers in this measure. Though Richler's transformation is the most dramatic, it does occur in the other writers. It is aptly illustrated by two passages from Atwood:

The world of Nature presented by Seton and Roberts is one in which the animal is always a victim. No matter how brave, cunning and strong he is, he will be killed eventually, either by other animals (which these authors don't seem to mind too much; it's part of the game) or by men. Seton, especially, reverses the Nature-as-Monster pattern in stories such as "Lobo," "The Springfield Fox" and "Redruff." Here it is man who is the threat and the villain: the animals suffer much more through men, with their snares, traps, chains and poisons, than they would through other animals who are at least quick. The amount of elegiac emotion expended over the furry corpses that litter the pages of Seton and Roberts suggest [*sic*] that "tragic" is the wrong word: "pathetic" would be a better one.

Atwood, Survival 75

Like the first Richler passage quoted above, this one has seven independent, seven rankshifted clauses. It has no coordinated added clauses in it. By contrast, consider the added clauses in the following:

I made my way back across the expanse of paper *and* peered around the corner in to the kitchenette. A peculiar odour greeted me — there seemed to be garbage bags in every corner, *and* the rest of the space was taken up by a large pots and kettles [*sic*], some clean, others not. . . . I stooped *and* began to skim the papers off the surface of the carpet, much as one would skim scum from a pond.

Atwood, Edible Woman 51

Once again, the second passage is an exaggeration, but it is illustrative.

The serial tendency indicated by the increase in added independent clauses appears to confine itself to the independent clause, for in five of our eight writers the total of coordinators used for purposes other than sentence-compounding *de*creases. Figure 3.5 shows that even though there are increases in the means for coordinators, they are far less than one would expect from Figure 3.4. Although there seems to be more compounding of independent clauses, there is less compounding in the novel — less *copia* — of everything else. Figure 3.6 shows that despite the enormous increase in sentence compounding (3.4) the pull of the fictive medium towards tidiness produces a period that is, on average, shorter. In keeping with the general processes of simplification and parataxis, the fiction samples show a 50% increase over the nonfiction in the total number of sentences without finite dependent clauses in them (Figure 3.7).

PREDICATION & CLAUSAL ARRAYS

With occasional exceptions, novels have tended to be more about actions than about states: it is usually some kind of human action, after all, that is the mainspring of the plot. Accordingly, as we might expect, the fictive medium has more transitive verbs (Figure 3.8) — 15% among the Brits and nearly 20% among the Canadians. This change does not occur at a uniform rate, but it does occur in all eight writers. At the same time, the mean number of passive constructions drops by roughly 25% (from 40–45 per sample to 30–33), so that there is an even more pronounced increase in transitive predicators in the active voice — (Figure 3.9). Also dropping is the number of *be*-form verb phrase heads — in both the British and the Canadian samples by over a quarter (Figure 3.10). Robertson Davies is one of Canada's more copious producers of generalizations and hence is always very high in *be*-form predicators.[4] Even Davies, writing as Dunny Ramsay (a character in many ways like unto his writer), can show a genre-to-genre drop in *be*-form verbs. We illustrate it below.

A century ago the reading population *was* much smaller than it *is* today, and the clerisy *was* still a recognizable and important element in it. The education of the clerisy *was* on a plan which stressed study of the Greek and Latin classics almost to the exclusion of everything else; such an education *was* narrow in matter, but very wide in scope; it developed taste and encouraged independent thought in minds with any aptitude for such things. It had its ridiculous side, and it developed certain snobberies. Dickens's Dr. Blimber *was* one kind of Victorian schoolmaster, and Mr. Curdle, who defined the dramatic unities as "a kind of universal dove-tailedness with regard to place and time," typifies Dr. Blimber's duller pupils. But that classical culture — even on the Curdle level — gave a coherence to the reading public.

Davies, *Voice from the Attic* 25

Nobody had time or pity for these minor characters in the drama; all public compassion *was* for Orph Wettenhall. What agonies of mind must he not have endured before taking his life! *Was* it not significant that he had launched himself into the hereafter apparently gazing upward at the large stuffed head of a moose he had shot a good forty years before! Who would have the heart to take his place on the deerhunt next autumn? When had there *been* his like for deftness and speed in skinning a buck? But of his ability in skinning a client little was said, except that he had obviously meant to restore the missing funds as soon as he could.

Davies, *Fifth Business* 146

In sum, even in Canada's most static first-rank novelist — i.e. in the one who deals most visibly in *states* — the style in fiction is more transitive, more active, more predicative, and even sometimes less static than in his expository prose.

An aspect of the less hypotactic, more paratactic style of fiction is the loss of relative and subordinate clauses. Figure 3.11 shows that the loss is substantial and that it occurs in all eight pairs of samples. Figure 3.12 suggests that most of this loss — perhaps 75% on the average — is accounted for by a drop in the relative clauses. Fiction, being an action medium, is more interested in *how* people do things (subordinate clause used adverbially) than it is in *who* they are (relative clause).[5] Once again, two passages from Richler can be suggestive:

On our street, a working-class street, we wanted to be boxers or, failing that, baseball pitchers. Bonus boys. Speaking for myself, I got so far as to train for the Golden Gloves when I unfortunately came up against a schoolmate called Manny, *who* was already fighting professionally, working in preliminaries under an alias in small towns. Manny had the unnerving habit of blowing his nose on his glove before swatting me. I still insist he didn't knock me out. Revolted, I fainted. In Montreal we had the example of Maxie Berger, *who* fought in the Garden and once went the distance with Ike Williams; and we also had our one and only Ziggy 'The Fireball' Freed, *who* would have been a star with the Athletics had Connie Mack not been such a lousy anti-semite.

Richler, *Hunting Tigers* 52

At the age of twelve Duddy discovered that smiling boys with autograph books could get in to hockey practises at the Forum. Getting in to see minor league teams like the Royals was a cinch; and, if you were quick or smart enough to hide in the toilet after the Royals had left the ice you could also get to see the Canadiens practise, and those were the years of Lach, Blake, and the great Maurice Richard. While they were on the ice the players' spare sticks, kept in a rack against the wall in a gangway leading into the passages out, were guarded by a thirteen-year-old stick boy. Duddy guessed that these sticks, each with a star player's name stencilled on it, would be treasured by many a fan.

Richler, *Duddy Kravitz* 56

Notice that Richler's tendency to collapse the relative clause into attributive nouns and appositives, strong already in the nonfiction, gets even stronger in *Duddy Kravitz*. Figure 3.12 suggests that something similar happens in other writers as well.

In word-class distributions — as in predication — the fictive medium bends an author's language in the direction of action: fewer *things*, more *activity*. In six of our eight authors, there is a major loss of nouns in the fiction sample (Figure 3.13). In the remaining two, Richler and Callaghan, the trend is opposite, and though the reason is wholly different in each case, it is wholly plausible. Richler calls his characters by name insistently in *Duddy Kravitz*, and in places in the book there are as many as 14 proper nouns to the page; hence the book is an exception to the pronominal thrust of the genre. With Callaghan, the explanation is equally simple: *That Summer in Paris* is a first-person account (heavy use of *I*), largely first-hand gossip about Great Writers with whom Callaghan was collocated (each of whom then becomes *he*), and it is one of the least nominal, most pronominal, of Callaghan's works. The flip side of the decline in nouns is shown in Figure 3.14 (pronouns), for seven of our eight writers, and a mean increase of roughly 20%. The combination of loss of nouns with increase of pronouns has a substantial effect on the noun:pronoun ratio (Figure 3.15). Consider Atwood:

> But the imagery of the poem casts a different light on the story. The Finger itself is an anthropomorphic form: it is at first "an overhang /, Crooked like a talon." This could be the talon of a bird, but later it is overtly humanoid: after the accident the narrator says, "Above us climbed the last joint of the Finger / Beckoning bleakly the wide indifferent sky." The sky may be indifferent, but the Finger isn't: it beckons, and in a sense it is the beckoning of the Finger that has lured David to his death. It isn't the only giant hand present: in the second section, another peak is "like a fist in an ocean of rock...." The Divine Mother's hands are scarcely extended in blessing.
>
> Atwood, *Survival* 57

I can imagine the expressions on their faces at the office when they hear. But I can't tell them yet, I'll have to keep my job there for a while longer. Till Peter is finished articling we'll need the money. We'll probably have to live in an apartment at first, but later we can have a real house, a permanent place; it will be worth the trouble to keep clean.

Meanwhile I should be doing something constructive instead

of sitting around like this. First I should revise the beer question-
naire and make out a report on my findings so I can type it up
first thing tomorrow and get it out of the way.

Then perhaps I'll wash my hair. And my room needs a general
clean-up. I should go through the dresser-drawers and throw out
whatever has accumulated in them, and there are some dresses
hanging in the closet I don't wear enough to keep. I'll give them
to the Salvation Army. Also a lot of costume jewellery, the kind
you get from relatives at Christmas: imitation gold pins in the
shapes of poodle dogs and bunches of flowers with pieces of
cut-glass for petals and eyes. There's a cardboard box full of
books, textbooks mostly, and letters from home I know I'll never
look again, and a couple of ancient dolls I've kept for sentimental
reasons.

Atwood, Edible Woman 105

The first passage contains 19 nouns, 4 pronouns; the second, 45 nouns
and 23 pronouns. This represents a shift of ratio from 4.75:1 to 1.96:1
— again a slight exaggeration, but only a slight one: the respective
figures for the samples *in toto* are 3.88:1 and 2.26:1. A further indicative
contrast between the two passages is that fiction interests itself in
character, hence in personhood; nonfiction, though not eschewing
character entirely, tends to describe rather than to depict it, and also
tends to focus on *things*. Not coincidentally the words immediately
following the first passage quoted above are "One thing . . . " The
four pronouns in the nonfiction passage above are four *its*; the fiction
passage is dominated by personal pronouns.

In general, one might expect fiction to be more ruthlessly edited
than nonfiction: much more is at stake word by word. Hence one
might also expect Modifier totals to drop from nonfiction to fiction.
We found that they do not drop; if anything they increase very
slightly. That they do so is not an interesting fact; what is interesting
is how the makeup of the "M" statistic changes from genre to genre.
In fiction, adjectives drop, while adverbs and function adverbs increase. These changes are illustrated in Figures 3.16 through 3.18. The
changes in adjectives, adverbs, and function adverbs are related to the
more nominal character of nonfiction and to the more predicative
character of fiction. The verb-modifying words increase along with
the verbs; the noun-modifying words decrease along with the nouns.
There is a drop in intensifiers in five of the eight writers, and a drop
in the mean number of intensifiers per sample from 21 to 16. Two

passages from Callaghan can give an illuminating glimpse of the change in modification from nonfiction to fiction:

> The Joyce apartment, at least the living (03) room in which we sat, upset me. Nothing looked right (03). In the whole (03) world there wasn't a more (33) original (03) writer than Joyce, the exotic (03) in the English (03) language. In the work he had on hand he was exploring the language of the dream world. In this room where he led his daily (03) life I must have expected to see some of the marks of his wild (03) imagination. Yet the place was conservatively (04) respectable (03). I was too (33) young (03) to have discovered then (34) that men with the most (33) daringly (04) original (03) minds are rarely (04) eccentric (03) in their clothes and their living (03) quarters.

Callaghan, That Summer in Paris 142

> She took three steps down the aisle, fearfully (04) aware (03) that many people were looking at her, and sat down, four rows from the back. Only (34) once (34) before (34) had she been in a strange (03) church. She unbuttoned her coat carefully (04), leaving a green (03) and black (03) scarf lying across her full (03) breasts, and relaxed in the seat, getting her big (03) body comfortable (03). Some one sat down beside her. The man with the gray (03) hair and red (03) face was sitting down beside her. She was annoyed because she knew she was too (33) definitely (04) aware (03) of him sitting beside her.

Callaghan, A Native Argosy 136–37

Modifier totals:	First Passage (17)	Second Passage (17)
Adj (03)	12	10
Adv (04)	2	3
Int (33)	2	1
F.A.(34)	1	3

The changes for each word-class fairly typify the general genre-to-genre shifts with respect to the modifying words.

Ex hypothesi, I said to myself reviewing all the numbers to this point in the chapter, the fiction samples should show a greater density of lexemes. The test of the hypothesis is given in Figure 3.19: they didn't. Only the works of Callaghan, Forster, Burgess, and Atwood show such an increase, and the trend among the other four is inconclusive. However, when one adds pronouns to the lexemes (Figure 3.20) — and pronouns are a borderline category anyway[6] — one can see the effects of the greater compression and tighter editing of fictive prose.

GENRE STYLE / AUTHOR STYLE

It would seem irrefutable from the figures in this chapter that, with or without a writer's assent, prose genre exerts several identifiable and definable pressures upon syntax in the process of composition. These pressures arise both from the differing kinds of material held in focus in the two genres and from differing ways — largely generically defined — of treating those different materials. Though we cannot say that a minimum degree of x or a maximum degree of y will form a threshold or ceiling that infallibly tells us whether a work is fiction or nonfiction prose, we can say that fiction almost infallibly moves a writer's everyday style in the direction of tidiness, parataxis, and action. Individual exceptions to the 20 general movements depicted in the figures to this chapter raise interesting questions — of which the most interesting are *why* and *to what effect*. We shall offer some answers to these questions in Part II, and the answers may differ from writer to writer.

Meanwhile, we should take note. The pull of genre is strong, but it is not so strong as the thrust of the writer's own linguistic identity: in the 20 figures in this chapter, there are 40 comparisons of nonfiction against fiction, 20 for the Brits and 20 for the Canadians. Though the right-hand bar is often in a different place from the left-hand bar, rank-orders from genre-to-genre are often fairly stable. A frequent exception to this is Atwood (Figures 3.5, 3.6, 3.15), who of all writers living today is probably the most self-conscious with regard to the kinds of grammatical phenomena that we have dealt with in this chapter. Atwood notwithstanding, identity seems to assert itself: writers of short independent clauses (Forster, Woolf, Callaghan) are likely to write short in both genres; writers of long independent clauses (Orwell, Burgess, Davies) are likely to write long in both. Those who summon the relative clause (Figure 3.12) will summon the relative clause, and those refraining will refrain. A similar process is seen again and again throughout all 20 figures. It is seen even though the measures selected for this chapter were specifically genre-sensitive. And though we have used several measures that are both genre- and writer-sensitive (relatives, 3.12, use of active voice, 3.9, noun: pronoun ratio, 3.15), we have not considered any that seem to be writer-sensitive only, such as sequencing and "D" value, among others. In sum what we are likely to see in prose is the opposite of what we are likely to see in the sonnet or the heroic couplet, wherein the genre dictates the most conspicuous formal features of the discourse, with less conspicuous features products of the individual writer. What we see (and hear) in the *syntax* of prose is most conspicuously the everyday voice of the writer, often unpremeditated and full of reflex, adapted first to written form and second to the imperatives of occasion and material.

NOTES

1. The *locus classicus* is Sir Philip Sidney's "Defence of Poesy." A somewhat more recent manifestation is in W.H. Sherman's *A Handbook of Literary Criticism*.

2. It may be, of course, that Wouk and Michener are working in a mixed genre — the propositional novel, namely a novel in which the propositional content is at least as important as any artistic consideration. The exhaustiveness with which Michener has researched nine-pounders like *Hawaii* and *Poland* suggests that this may be the case.

3. Davies becomes a special instance here for two reasons: 1) like Carlyle, he trained himself to write in an ostentatiously deviant style, only in Davies's case the disjunction is mainly temporal (18th and early 19th century) rather than mainly geographic as in Carlyle, who was deliberately trying to Aryanize and deFrancify English; 2) Though Intuitive Dunny Ramsay and Thinker David Staunton may differ in their typology, they both use the language in a way that is remarkably similar to that of Davies. Those three people (two fictive, one living) are among the very few small-town Ontarions in the last 20 years to employ the phrase "I dare say" other than in jest. See chapter 5, *infra*.

4. Though the *be*-form predicator does indeed see many specific uses (e.g. He *is* my uncle), its presence seems to be an almost infallible index of a high level of generalization. Others, besides Davies, to show abnormally high counts of *be*-form predictors include Philip Sidney, Ben Jonson, Samuel Johnson, Matthew Arnold, Joseph Conrad, Gertrude Stein, and G.K. Chesterton: generalizers all.

5. An interesting case in this connexion is that of Hemingway, who was so wedded to the values of fiction that he often used an *if* clause where meaning would better support a *who* clause. See *Death in the Afternoon* 192: "If a writer . . ." quoted in chapter 4, *infra* 88–89.

6. The ambiguity arises from the fact that pronouns have declension and hence violate the third of the three criteria by which function words are defined: 1) they are finite in number; 2) they require context in order to "mean"; 3) they are not normally inflected.

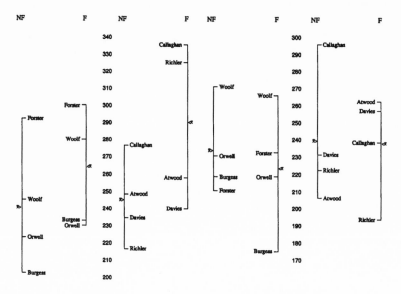

FIGURE 3.1
Independent Clauses per Sample

FIGURE 3.2
Rankshifted Clauses per Sample

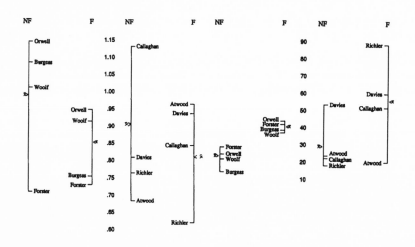

FIGURE 3.3
Rankshifted Clauses per
Independent Clause

FIGURE 3.4
And/or – *Added*
Independent Clauses

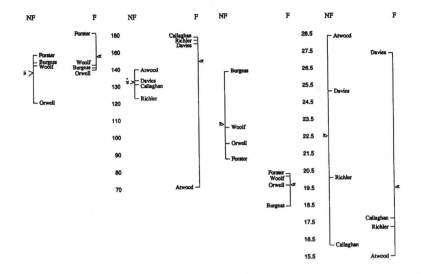

FIGURE 3.5
Coordinators (41)

FIGURE 3.6
Average Period Length

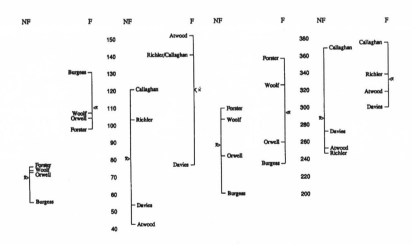

FIGURE 3.7
*Periods per Sample with no
Subordinator (42) or Relative (43)*

FIGURE 3.8
Finite Transitive Predicators (02)

71

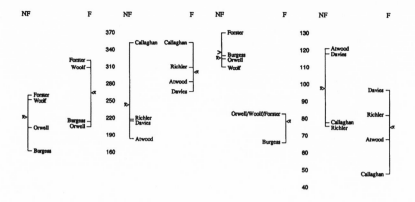

FIGURE 3.9
Active Voice Finite
Transitive Predicators (02-022)

FIGURE 3.10
Be *Finite Predicators (213)*

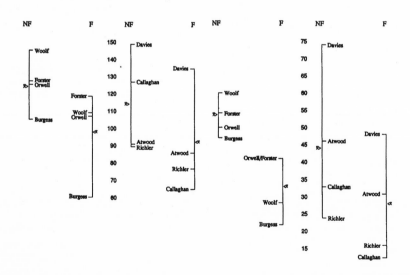

FIGURE 3.11
Subordinators and Relatives
(42 + 43)

FIGURE 3.12
Relatives (43)

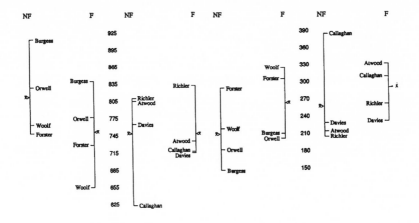

FIGURE 3.13
Nouns (01)

FIGURE 3.14
Pronouns (11)

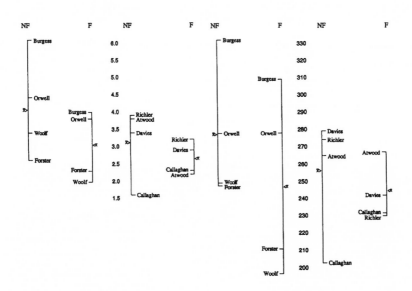

FIGURE 3.15
Noun : Pronoun Ratio (01 : 11)

FIGURE 3.16
Adjectives (03)

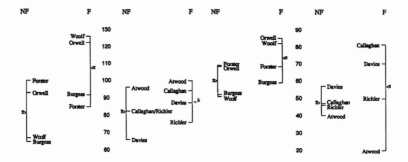

FIGURE 3.17
Function Adverbs (34)

FIGURE 3.18
Lexical Adverbs (04)

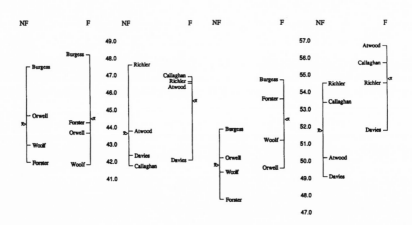

FIGURE 3.19
Lexemes
(01 + 02 + 03 + 04 + 05 + 06 + 07)

FIGURE 3.20
Lexemes plus Pronouns (11)

74

SECTION — Writers

Part 2.0

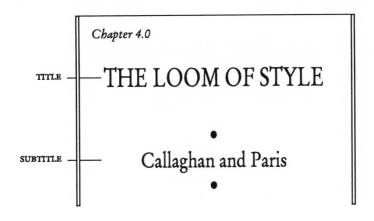

THE LOOM OF STYLE

•

Callaghan and Paris

•

Morley Callaghan is probably the first native-born Canadian writer to have made it as an object of discussion in literary salons in New York and Paris.[1] Often viewed by non-Canadians as a kind of lesser Hemingway,[2] he was even promoted, by one American reviewer (Chamberlain), to American status as one of the "athletic" American writers ("hard and compact, telling, pugilistic") whose sensibilities had been formed in journalism — writers like Ring Lardner and Hemingway. Despite his physical collocation in Paris with all those Americans and despite his early publishing allegiances to Charles Scribner, Maxwell Perkins,[3] and Harold Ross,[4] he seems increasingly to be regarded north of the border as an Authentic Canadian. In her book in the M & S Canadian Writers series, Patricia Morley is at some pains to demonstrate that he is a *Toronto* writer and therefore the genuine Canadian article.

This question — Canadian or alien? — is recurrent in the Callaghan criticism. It is related to a second, and to me more important, question: namely, what are the specific features of the Callaghan style? Without a clear answer to the second question, we cannot begin to answer the first. From day one he has been known for his style, instantly and universally recognized for both plainness and clarity, and nearly all of his critics have felt obliged to make mention of his manner of using language.

Hoar uses the term "American Anglo-Saxon" for Callaghan's language, calling it "mundane, almost quaint" (8). Woodcock says that Callaghan had come to the conclusion that

> in our age at least — writing must be uncomplicated and direct. It should present the object — not seek to transform it into something else or use something else to suggest or describe it. (25)

Elsewhere Woodcock speaks of "his ideal of stark, direct statement" (27), "[in *Strange Fugitive*] the narrative style is simple and for the most part decorated only by a frequent use of the vernacular." "Stripping language . . . seeing things as they are and using writing to make statements about them" form the core of his aesthetic. When things are working well for Callaghan, Woodcock gives him praise for "simplicity and economy of writing" (37) and for "freshness and honesty and directness" (39). W.J. Keith says "he is known for the lucid simplicity of his style, for direct language without frills or snags" (128). Patricia Morley, speaking of *A Native Argosy*, says

> The style here, more than in the novels, reflects a concern for spare, simple language and syntax. His early ideal was to show the object freshly and simply. Tell the truth cleanly, he advises: no big words, no metaphysics, no "escape into metaphor"; the words should be "as transparent as glass." (51)

There is, in short, an overwhelming consensus that Callaghan wrote (and still writes) in some variety of plain, that he was devoted to stripping excess from language, that he was generally successful in his avowed detestation of artifice and metaphysics. In this respect his reputation is like that of Hemingway, though he has had no Harry Levin, Gutwinski, or Peterson, to flesh out the specific traits of his style.

Also notably similar to the case of Hemingway is the fact that Callaghan's pronouncements on style and language have consistently reinforced the views expressed by his critics: he is a resolute *preacher* of plain style values as well as being a perceived *practitioner* of them. He has specifically rejected "show-off writers," has spoken of his "hatred of standard smooth mediocrity." "It was part of my writing creed," he says (*That Summer* 75), "to distrust calculated charm in prose." Other statements, quoted below, reinforce these views.

Partly because of Hemingway's eminence as the alleged fountainhead of the Plain American Style and partly because of shared publishers, shared employers (*Toronto Star*), and shared times in Paris in the 1920s, Callaghan has been insistently linked to Hemingway. Because Hemingway was older and found success and fame sooner, perhaps also because he comes from a larger and more domineering country, Hemingway has often been regarded as the influencer, Callaghan as the influenced — even in Canada. The most vocal Canadian propagator of the latter notion is Fraser Sutherland, whose book, *The Style of Innocence*, deals with every aspect of their relationship except what might be visible in the particulars of style. Patricia Morley has said, without documentation, "Callaghan deplores the myth linking his work to Hemingway's," and she continues, without presentation of any stylistic evidence, "contrary to Fraser Sutherland's thesis . . . I would argue that the link was never stylistic."

Callaghan himself on this point does not deny strong affinity. Near the end of *That Summer in Paris*, he writes of Hemingway:

> Then he became very talkative about writing. He talked about style, and we were in happy and splendid agreement. The decorative style, the baroque based on a literary adornment of perceptions, was an affectation in our time, he said. Only the clear direct stripped statement belonged to our time, and it wasn't just a matter of what you could or couldn't do. (233–34)

We were in happy and splendid agreement. That is far from a rejection of the notion of a large common ground in matters stylistic. At the same time, the connexion — with Hemingway the dominant figure — has bothered Callaghan:

> When I went again to New York at the time *Strange Fugitive* came out, the business manager at Scribner's, Whitney Darrow, who took me out to dinner, told me with enthusiasm that in their promotion of my novel they had tied me up with Hemingway. A success with *The Sun Also Rises*? All right, tie me in with that success, you understand? Oh, they certainly did! And the mill run of reviewers picked up the cue.
>
> Later . . . Max Perkins told me earnestly . . . it had never been his idea to associate me and my work with Hemingway. From the beginning he had seen that I had entirely different perceptions.
>
> But at the time of my launching I was bewildered and hurt. . . .

Suddenly the reviewers were hitting me on the head in Hemingway's name. Nor could I expect Hemingway to send up smoke signals explaining that three years ago he had read as many of my stories as I had of his. Yet I knew it couldn't embarrass me, meeting Ernest as meet him now I surely would. (*That Summer in Paris* 63–64)

There is, of course, no conflict between "entirely different purposes" and strong affinities of style: the same style, or similar styles, can be turned to different ends, and two writers sharing the same aesthetic can produce markedly different styles.

Thus we return to our two initial questions: 1) Is Callaghan Canadian or alien (and, if alien, how much influenced by Anderson, Hemingway, and Stein); and 2) what are the precise characteristics of the Callaghan style? It is with the second question that we shall begin.

THE STYLE

The history of style is littered with instances of writers who talked plain, praising the plain style, and often wrote fancy — Thomas Sprat, Jonathan Swift, and Ernest Hemingway to name only three. It is also full of cases of those who talked the plain style game and were as good as their word — Ben Jonson, John Bunyan, and Somerset Maugham, to name three more. It is with the Jonsonian group that Callaghan belongs: though his remarks on style do not constitute a handbook for the style itself, there is surely no conflict between the precepts and the style, and the style of the Paris Callaghan is in several measures the plainest style of its time.

We have selected three works for scrutiny: the two earliest fiction works, *Strange Fugitive* and *A Native Argosy*, and the later work of nonfiction that looks back to the period of writing and publication of the other two — *That Summer in Paris*. There are good reasons for the selection. The stereotype of the Callaghan style ("muscular, terse, and Hemingwayesque") was conceived and propagated — in the Scribner's publicity office to be sure — on the basis of those two early works. *Strange Fugitive*, as Woodcock has said, is "a textbook example of his writing theory carried into practice" (27). The selection of

That Summer in Paris is similarly obvious; not only does it illuminate the other two works, but it offers some tests of the durability of the early style. It goes, moreover, well beyond a reminiscence about the times and about the intimates like Ernest and Scott and Robert McAlmon and the numerous less-intimates; it serves, *en passant*, as a kind of *credo auctoris*, from which 95% of the nuggets in critical treatments of Callaghan's theories have been plucked.

The samples to be used in my discussion of Callaghan's style are listed in Table 4.1. We have picked three Americans alleged to be close to Callaghan in stylistic theory and practice (Stein, Hemingway, Anderson), plus three notable Brits who rejected the ornateness of the Victorians (Forster, Woolf, Orwell). In addition we have selected six Canadians and four internationals born within two decades of Callaghan.

TABLE 4.1

Samples Used for Chapter 4

NONFICTION	FICTION
Callaghan, *That Summer in Paris*	Callaghan, *Native Argosy/ Strange Fugitive*
Hemingway, *Death in the Afternoon*	Forster, *Passage to India*
Anderson, *A Storyteller's Story*	Faulkner, *As I Lay Dying*
Stein, *Paris France*	Grove, *Fruits of the Earth*
Woolf, *The Common Reader (II)*	MacLennan, *Two Solitudes*
Davies, *A Voice from the Attic*	Orwell, *1984*
Waugh, *A Little Learning*	Nabokov, *Lolita*
Frye, *Fables of Identity*	Fitzgerald, *Tender Is the Night*
Woodcock, *The Rejection of Politics*	Ostenso, *Wild Geese*

Sentences & Clauses

"Some variety of plain" begins in Callaghan's case with a propensity for the short sentence — several decades, in fact, ahead of its time (Figure 4.1). With that comes a propensity for the short independent clause (Figures 4.2 and 4.3) — roughly two-thirds the length of the independent clause of Stein and Hemingway, and barely half the length (on the fiction side) of that of Callaghan's contemporary, the eminent plain talker George Orwell.

These independent clauses are apt to be set in paratactic rows,[6] often in the fiction samples in compound sentences but in the nonfiction with more terminal punctuation and fewer coordinators. The sentence — compound or simple — without finite dependent clauses in it is Callaghan's overwhelming favourite (Figure 4.4); such a sentence represents 120 of the 210 sentences of the *TSIP* sample and 143 of the 196 sentences of the fiction sample (57% and 73% respectively, each number tops for its genre). Two illustrations are suggestive:

Then Ernest told us about the new baby and asked if we wouldn't like to come to his house and see the boy. We told him we would. We were at ease. Within a few minutes I had felt all my old liking for him.

That Summer in Paris 96

He told Jimmie Nash about the Labor Temple, but Jimmie would consider only the political side of it and was cynical of Harry's talk of strength. Vera was not even interested. Harry quarrelled with her because she would not promise to go with him to the Temple. Respectable people did not go there, she said. They quarrelled and he said she was preventing him from living in his own way.

Strange Fugitive 49

Both passages are representative of their samples with respect to simple and compound sentences: the complex and the compound-complex sentence are in the minority. We should note (in passing) in the fiction passage the tendency towards repetition of words: *Temple-Temple*, *quarrel-quarrel*, and *go-go*. It is a hallmark of what Harry Mencken called "the bold, bad style of the Cafe Dôme," a hallmark that is imprinted upon the styles of Stein, Anderson, Hemingway, and Callaghan.

Callaghan's consistent and lifelong preference for the simple and the compound sentence did not prevent him from admitting two changes into the style of *That Summer in Paris*: 1) a major reduction in *and-* and *or*-added independent clauses (from 74 to 22 in the York samples), and 2) a major increase in the number of finite dependent clauses (from 88 to 170). Both measures would have shown change as an effect of genre, but only to the extent of a third to a half what we see in this comparison. What are the reasons? Simple change of the writer's preference could alter the compounding, as this is one of the easiest changes to make in one's style: that of cutting a conjunction, then adding a period and a capital letter. Perhaps parodists and reviewers, attacking the *faux-naif* conjunctive style of the 1920s, elevated some consciousness in this regard. The second change — the notable increase in finite dependent clauses — curiously does not much affect Callaghan's insistent preference for the simple and the compound sentence as opposed to the complex. What it does seem to do is to increase the density of dependent clauses within the complex sentences themselves. For example:

> As we drank our beer I noticed that Ernest would empty his glass in a few gulps, then turn to me . . . Though I kept my half-filled glass in my hand, and Ernest could see it was still half-filled, each time he ordered he would say, "Are you sure you won't have one?" The waiter leaves the saucer that comes with each drink on the table, so he can count them up for you when you are leaving and show you what you owe him.
>
> *That Summer in Paris* 96

There is nothing equivalently complex in the early fiction: ten finite dependent clauses in four sentences (the three dots indicate a compound sentence omitted). Even though in the later work he wrote a more complex sentence when he wrote a complex sentence, his utterance of choice remained simple or compound.

Similarly durable is his affection for the nonfinite verbs — roughly seven nonfinite clauses for every ten periods. He is at the top of the scale in both genres (Figure 4.5). Examples of his fondness for this specifically economizing device are everywhere. For example (infinitives=05, participles=06, gerunds= 07):

> Often he would be looking out the window, leaving (06) me alone and waiting (06). It struck me, watching (06) him, that maybe he wore his hat in the office and maybe went hatless outside. Wary as I was, I knew immediately I could trust him. While apparently fumbling (07) around rather awkwardly with his words he was getting some kind of a sharp impression of me. All right, there I was, let him go (05) ahead.
>
> *That Summer in Paris* 59

A preference for the nonfinite verb forms has been called "conversational" and "modern" by Louis T. Milic. It has been demonstrated to be the latter, at least in the participles (*Prose Style* 237–42).

It clearly is economizing — reducing as it does the size of dependent elements — and as such it is wholly in keeping with Callaghan's avowed objective of writing plain, clean, stripped prose.

Predication

A writer who produces so many independent clauses and so many nonfinite clauses should, *ex hypothesi*, produce relatively many predicators of all kinds — if, that is, his distribution of copula, passive, and active is normal for his time. But Callaghan's distribution of these verb types is not normal, as we can see by Figures 4.6, 4.7, and 4.8. He eschews the "dead" verb forms, the copula and the passive, preferring active forms, verbs of action, at all times.

In addition, he has a strong preference for direct predication — for placing the predicator immediately after the head of the subject phrase, without intervening qualification or intervening adverbial matter. Our test for such a preference is in a count of all three-class patterns involving a determiner-noun-verb sequence (31-01-02 and 31-01-21) and of all three-class patterns opening with a pronoun followed by a verb (11-02-xx and 11-21-xx). As Figure 4.9 shows, among the (roughly contemporary) writers here, Callaghan has by far the strongest propensity for use of this device.[7] We can consider it below, operating together with his drive towards both active verbs and nonfinite clauses (Verb markings: A=active; P=passive; C=copula; F=finite; N=nonfinite):

He refused (AF) to go (AN) to parties with Stan Farrel for fear of meeting (AN) people who knew (AF) him. He wanted (AF) to be (CN) alone, taking (AN) long walks, thinking (AN) always of himself, at times walking (AN) rapidly, his hands clenched (PN). One Sunday evening he wandered (AF) into the Labor Temple and was at first amused (PF) at the meeting, then imagined (AF) himself making (AN) a speech on the platform.

Strange Fugitive 46

Notice that of the passage's 14 verbs, the actives outnumber the passives and the copulas by a ratio of 11:3 — almost exactly representative of the 450:120 ratio for the sample as a whole. Of the six finite verbs, four are parts of direct predications; the only two that are not are the two last finite verb phrases (*was amused, imagined*), both of them predicators of minus-additioned clauses. The density of nonfinites in this passage is overwhelming. These grammatical devices — active and nonfinite verbs, direct predication — join with repetitious use of lexemes (even in this short passage, *meeting-meeting* and *walks-walking*) to be major constituents of the stripped, clean, plain Callaghan style.

Both from the three works sampled here and from a reading of his other writing, Callaghan seems a heavily pronominal writer. Figure 4.10 bears this out. He is particularly given to pronoun in subject function, often in initial position in sentence or clause (Figure 4.11), and very often we see the same pronoun-subject for several sentences running:

> They lined up and got their hats from the check-room. They had to line up to get out. They watched the two girls who were a little tight earlier in the evening, and who now seemed quite drunk.

Strange Fugitive 94

This tendency to write "focused" prose — in which the same subject appears in a series of three to seven consecutive clauses — is another aspect of Callaghan's drive towards plainness.

Word Classes, Phrase Groups, Modification

The plain short sentence, the plain short clause, the paratactic string, the unadorned subject-predicator clause opening, the basically active and predicative drive of the style itself — these could all be said to be operating mainly at clause or sentence level, and they bend the language frame in the direction of its *verb* (as opposed to *noun*) component. Things work at the phrase level, too, to bend the language frame in the same direction. For example, over half of Callaghan's prepositional phrases are used adverbially rather than as modifiers of nouns or pronouns. As Figure 4.12 shows, this is unusual, it being normal for the noun-modifying prepositional phrases to dominate by 4:3 or more rather than to be in the minority. Callaghan's tendency here is related to another tendency: to eschew things normally used in noun phrases as qualifiers of the head — not only the prepositional phrase but the relative clause. Figure 4.18 shows a very low ratio of noun-modifying prepositional phrases to nouns (e.g. the man *at the bar*, people *of good taste*, houses *of timber and stucco*). His avoidance of the relative clause is even more pronounced: in both genres is he not only low in absolute number of relative clauses (Figure 4.13) but is very low in relative clauses as a percentage of all finite rankshifted clauses (Figure 4.14). "The living room in which we sat" (Joyce's — *That Summer in Paris* 142) is a rare kind of construction in Callaghan.

He also avoids the adjectivally modified noun phrase (31-03-01: the *big* house, the *difficult* passage); in most of the Inventory's samples such phrases will occur between 80 and 120 times. It is a favourite of the more descriptive Victorians, as well as of descriptive writers such as Fitzgerald and Nabokov. Note that Callaghan keeps this one on a very short leash (Figure 4.15), and indeed is generally suppressive of adjectives (Figure 4.16). At the same time, his ratio of adverbs to adjectives (Figure 4.17) is higher than that of any other writer used in the chapter except for the three Paris salon-mates from the *rue de Fleurus*.

Group Style & Influence

The weakness of Fraser Sutherland's book is that it does not say much about style: he moves from biographical data to text in a single leap. But, whatever its shortcomings as stylistic analysis, the book might well be grounded on a sound hunch. Whether Hemingway's style formed a paradigm for Callaghan's, or Callaghan's for Hemingway's, or Anderson's for the styles of both, or Stein's precepts by way of Anderson's practice . . . whatever the case and whichever way the influences went, these four literary celebrities of the 1920s were close to one another in theory and in many aspects of their practice. Influence in style as in politics, though perhaps pervasive, is always difficult to prove, and the critics who spend large amounts of time on the subject could probably use that time better elsewhere. But clearly these four writers had much in common.

Consider the nonfiction side of any of this chapter's Figures from 4.6 through 4.18. Though Stein is an occasional exception and though Anderson is usually less close to Callaghan than the other two are, it is insistently Hemingway, Stein, and Anderson that are closest to

Callaghan. They all deviate from the same norms in the same direction. Note particularly Figure 4.17. They are all predicative, pronominal, adjective-suppressive writers, with all except Stein relying heavily on the nonfinite predicators for compression and "naturalness" of tone. On the lexical side, all of them tend to fasten on to key lexemes and use them repeatedly. In the 18 years' research involved in the York Inventory of Prose Style, we have never found a group of stylists with as much in common as these four have; the only case even remotely similar is that of Addison and Steele, and two is hardly a group, though the interchange between them may well have had much in common with the interchange among these Paris four.

I have severe doubts that Hemingway and Callaghan, or either of them with Stein or Anderson, ever sat around talking about removal of nouns, suppression of adjectives, or foregrounding of the predicative elements in the language: writers do not talk about style in the way that rhetoricians or linguists do.[8] As Stein said later of Hemingway, one of Ernest's great charms was that he just did it (imitation, that is) without consciously knowing what he was doing.[9] No doubt all of them talked to one another about the bare stripped statement and learned much from each other about how to do it well and truly. In Callaghan's account, the critical vocabulary in which they discussed style had perjorative terms like *fine writing, educated, show-off, brilliant phrase, calculated charm, decorative, baroque, affectation,* and *literary adornment.* Its favourable terms were things like *plain, transparent, clear, direct, clean, stripped, authentic, true/truly,* and *revealing the object as it was.* (Every generation, of course, wants to tell it like it is.)

They did have a program, even though its articulation might have been either fragmentary or grasped only intuitively. That program, in sum, might be expressed as follows: 1) Elevate the action component of the language and suppress all that is passive or static; 2) focus sentences tightly on concrete things or concrete people; 3) annihilate elegant variation (especially of nominals) because it adds words without adding effect — if you used a good word the first time, don't be afraid to use it again; 4) cultivate the sounds and rhythms of natural speech. The last of these was especially embraced by Callaghan, with his heavy reliance on nonfinite verbs and on turns of vernacular speech.

I know very little of stylistic influence or of how to trace it. But it does seem to me that the role of Anderson in this group has probably been, of late, given less than its due. Of Hemingway, Gertrude Stein said "He was formed by them" (Stein and Anderson) (*Autobiography* 265). And Callaghan himself said, "I was grateful to Anderson" (*That Summer in Paris* 48), recalling a page later that at a Greenwich Village party he introduced himself to Anderson by saying (not entirely playfully) "You're my father" (*That Summer in Paris* 49). There is not much doubt that Anderson, Stein, and Callaghan were all dismayed when Hemingway rose and smote Anderson publicly with the publication of *The Torrents of Spring*, a nasty satire of the *faux-naif* Andersonian style. But, as Stein later observed, the reason Hemingway could write such a parody was that he had spent long years learning the very techniques that he exaggerated in the parody.

In places, the community of utterance about style between Callaghan and Hemingway is as strong as the community of stylistic emphasis. Writing in the early 1960s, Callaghan said:

> The popular writers of the day like Hergesheimer, Edith Wharton, James Branch Cabell, Galsworthy, Hugh Walpole, H.G. Wells — except for *Tono Bungay* — I had rejected fiercely. Show-off writers; writers intent on proving to their readers that they could be clever and had some education, I would think. Such vanities should be beneath them if they were really concerned in revealing the object as it was . . .
> . . . Writing had to do with the right relationship between the words and the thing or person being described: the words should be as transparent as glass, and every time a writer used a brilliant phrase to prove himself witty or clever he merely took the mind of the reader away from the object and directed it to himself; he became simply a performer.
>
> *That Summer in Paris* 19, 21

In an attack on Aldous Huxley three decades earlier, Hemingway had put a very similar set of thoughts this way:

> When writing a novel a writer should create living people; people not characters. A *character* is a caricature. If a writer can make people live there may be no great characters in his book, but it is possible that his book will remain as a whole; as an entity; as a novel. If the people the writer is making talk of old masters; of music; of modern painting; or letters; or of science then they should talk of those subjects in the novel. If they do not talk of those subjects and the writer makes them talk of them he is a faker, and if he talks about them himself to show how much he

knows then he is showing off. No matter how good a phrase or a simile he may have if he puts it in where it is not absolutely necessary and irreplaceable he is spoiling his work for egotism. Prose is architecture, not interior decoration, and the Baroque is over. For a writer to put his own intellectual musings, which he might sell for a low price as essays, into the mouths of artificially constructed *characters* is good economics, perhaps, but does not make literature. . . . If a writer of prose knows enough about what he is writing about he may omit things that he knows and the reader, if the writer is writing truly enough, will have a feeling of those things as strongly as though the writer had stated them. . . . A writer who omits things because he does not know them only makes hollow places in his writing. A writer who appreciates the seriousness of writing so little that he is anxious to make people see he is formally educated, cultured, or well-bred is merely a popinjay . . . A serious writer is not to be confounded with a solemn writer. A serious writer may be a hawk or a buzzard or even a popinjay, but a solemn writer is always a bloody owl

Death in the Afternoon 191–92

Now: Who influenced whom? That is not for me to say. I should only like to point out the community of values and the community of vocabulary. More than chance is required to produce such similarities.

As for the question about Callaghan with which we began the chapter — Canadian or alien? — it seems to me wrong to phrase it as an *either/or* question. Just as in heritage he is clearly Irish and Roman Catholic, so in setting and theme and temperament he is clearly Canadian. But his early literary associations were almost wholly American, and so was the Callaghan style before he was into his mid-twenties. W.J. Keith has put it this way:

He had no need to search for America since he lives and writes totally within the American grain, his early work appearing in the United States alongside Hemingway, Sherwood Anderson, and Sinclair Lewis. Indeed, his was the first sustained body of fiction in Canada that deliberately associated itself with American rather than European assumptions and traditions. (127–28)

Now, to be sure, his Paris colleagues could have learned just as much from him as he learned from them, and in the end he might have made just as much of an imprint on that Paris-American Plain Style as anyone else did. But the style of his early fiction, like the backers and

promoters of that fiction in the book trade, was most closely associated with the American literary community, notably the expatriate
wing of that community.

That style seems to have been durable. Few are the differences
between the style of the two early fiction works and the style of *That
Summer in Paris*: the compounding is dramatically cut, and the
tight-fisted restraint on finite subordinate clauses is much relaxed.
But, these apart, the terse voice of the early Callaghan was still very
much the voice of the mature artist in 1962. In the post-1950 fiction,
we encounter more figurative language than in the fiction early. But
the syntactic frame — the loom on which Callaghan has woven his
words — remains the one that was sized and shaped in the 1920s.

NOTES

1. Though several Canadians (e.g. Service and Roberts) had enjoyed attention
from U.S. audiences, Callaghan was probably first to make it as a salon figure.

2. *Vide infra*: p. 86 ff.

3. Perkins was Editor-in-Chief of Scribner's, publisher of Callaghan's first two
books.

4. Ross, legendary head wallah of *The New Yorker*, published many Callaghan stories from the 1920s until the onset of World War II.

5. In *Morley Callaghan* 31–33 and elsewhere *passim*, Brandon Conron tries to
refute a Hemingway–Callaghan connexion, both aesthetic and stylistic. Not
convincing.

6. Between the early fiction and *That Summer in Paris*, Callaghan cut back
on the compounding of clauses with *and*. But his tendency towards parataxis was
durable.

7. A comparison with Figure 7.10 is interesting: Even against the much more
recent, much more "contemporary" control samples of the Atwood chapter,
Callaghan remains formidably high in numerical density of direct predication —
much higher than Atwood. However, because of his greater propensity for
minus-additioning of independent clauses, direct predication as a percentage of
all finite predicators ends up lower for Callaghan than for Atwood.

8. A decade and a half later, in *Lectures in America*, Stein was to make a highly
explicit statement of the values of the Paris-American style without any reference
to Anderson, Hemingway, or Callaghan:

Adjectives are not really and truly interesting. In a way anybody can know
always has known that, because after all adjectives effect nouns and as nouns
are not really interesting the thing that effects a not too interesting thing is
of necessity not interesting. In a way as I say anybody knows that because
of course the first thing that anybody takes out of anybody's writing are
the adjectives . . . .

Verbs and adverbs are more interesting. In the first place they can be so mistaken. It is wonderful the number of mistakes a verb can make and that is equally true of its adverb. Nouns and adjectives never can make mistakes can never be mistaken but verbs can be so endlessly, both as to what they do and how they agree or disagree with whatever they do. The same is true of adverbs.

In that way any one can see that verbs and adverbs are more interesting than nouns and adjectives. (133)

Narrow minds might find fault with Stein's logic, but that is beside the point: the aesthetic of language is clear and is clearly represented in the styles of Stein, Anderson, Hemingway, and Callaghan.

9. In *The Autobiography of Alice B. Toklas* 266, Gertrude Stein says of Hemingway, "... he is such a good pupil ... it is so flattering to have a pupil who does it without understanding it, in other words he takes training and anybody who takes training is a favorite pupil."

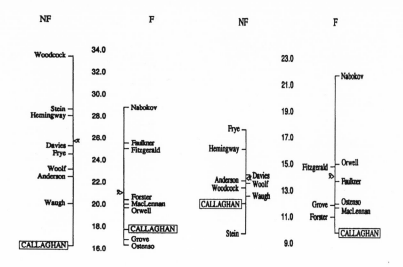

FIGURE 4.1
Average Period Length

FIGURE 4.2
*Average Independent
Clause Length*

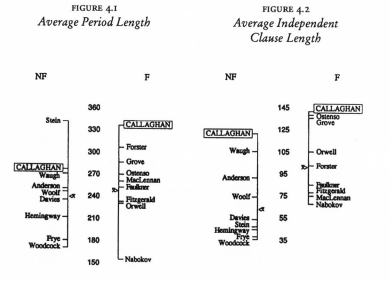

FIGURE 4.3
Independent Clauses per Sample

FIGURE 4.4
*Periods per Sample with no
Subordinator (42) or Relative (43)*

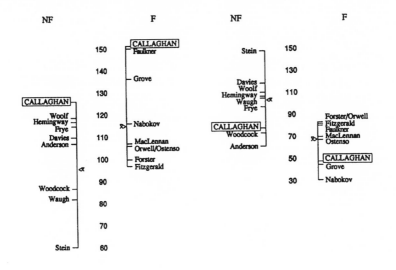

FIGURE 4.5
Nonfinite Clauses
(05 + 06 + 07)

FIGURE 4.6
Be *Finite Predicators (213)*

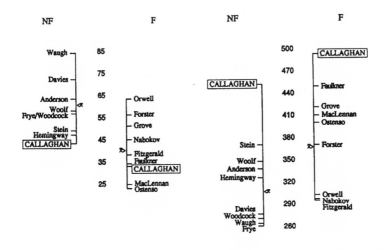

FIGURE 4.7
Passive Predications
(022 + 052 + 062 + 072)

FIGURE 4.8
Active Constructions (Nonfinites
included) (021 + 051 + 061 + 071)

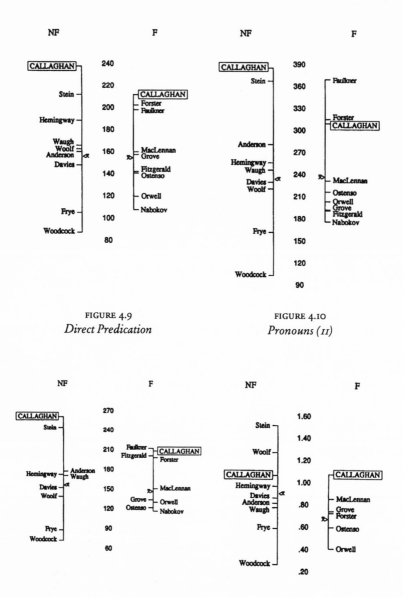

FIGURE 4.9
Direct Predication

FIGURE 4.10
Pronouns (11)

FIGURE 4.11
Pronoun Subjects (115)

FIGURE 4.12
Adverbial Prepositional Phrases:
Noun-modifying Prepositional Phrases

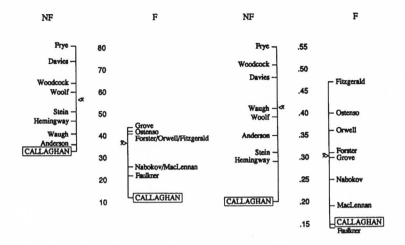

FIGURE 4.13
Relatives (43)

FIGURE 4.14
Relative Clauses as %
of all Finite Clauses

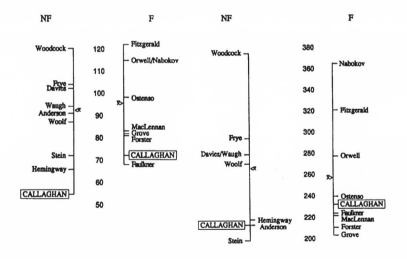

FIGURE 4.15
Determiner – Adjective – Noun
(31-03-01)

FIGURE 4.16
Adjectives (03)

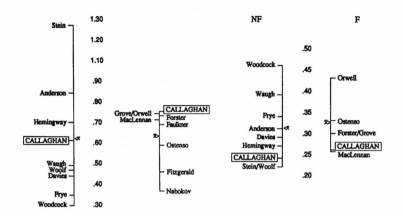

FIGURE 4.17
*Adverbs + Function Adverbs
as % of Adjectives*

FIGURE 4.18
*Noun-modifying Prepositions : Noun
— Ratio (511 : 01)*

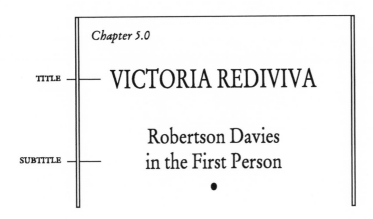

Chapter 5.0

TITLE — **VICTORIA REDIVIVA**

SUBTITLE — Robertson Davies
in the First Person

•

Robertson Davies is collocated here with Morley Callaghan as an accident of their births: in this study, they come in chronological succession. But that is almost the only way in which they touch. Callaghan's public *persona* is as insistently ordinary as the characters of his early fiction; Davies's *persona* is ornate and theatrically enigmatic. Callaghan's sources, places, and influences are native and North American; Davies's are not nearly so parochial. To Davies, unlike Callaghan, there is no such entity as "the thing itself"; whatever else the "thing" is, it is the embodiment of archetype, allegory, message. The styles, too, are as we might expect: polar opposites. So, onward to the next pole!

> There is no democracy in the world of intellect, and no democracy of taste. Great efforts have been made to pretend that this is not so, but they have failed. (*Vox* 24)[1]

Much of the commitment to things intellectual and to things undemocratic and elitist noted by Peterman is in that pair of sentences above, and so, of course, is much of the Davies style: the compound sentence with its antiquated resonances, the reliance on *be*-forms in the predicators — signs of generalization — the reasoning by counter-assertion rather than by logic or evidence ("they have failed"). Nearly everything is there, in shorthand form, except some of the details of his most habitual syntax and one major recurrent lexical field (religion and religious mystery). Those two sentences show us a lot, and not least of what they show us is that Davies, with a gift for focusing his energies like that of Austen and other great artists, can pack a lot of behaviour into a short compass of space.

But a great artist deserves a longer and more leisured look. After all, scholars and critics have spilt a lot of ink on assessments of his work. His style, *per se*, has not generally been singled out as an object of attention — certainly not to the degree of Callaghan's. In Davies's case, the Callaghan paradox (many critics taking up his style but very few really dealing with it) is inverted: in an examination of the Davies bibliography, I could find but one article that claimed to deal specifically with his style, and that my 1977 prolusion for this chapter.

Yet Cude, Bonnycastle, and Peterman — all dealing ostensibly with nonstylistic features of his work — each grapple interestingly and intelligently with stylistic aspects of these texts. There may be excellent reasons for this fact: first, that "in Davies's books the language alone is sufficient to make them compulsively readable" (Heintzman 2); second, that Davies seems to have put more work and more conscious thought to the uses of language than any other living Canadian writer except Atwood; third, in Davies both as self and as artist, "form and substance come together" (Bonnycastle 21–40) to make a nearly monistic whole. Davies's concern with and use of language have not gotten a long shrift from the critics but they have gotten a pretty good one.

Cude ("Historiography" 48–67) focuses less on the style of Davies than on that of Dunny Ramsay, but he makes revealing observations on the recursive lexis of avarice and what it discloses about character, and he shrewdly assesses Dunny's manipulation of language for glossing and glozing his most unseemly moments of moral weakness. Peterman, in his workmanlike survey of Davies's life and career, does not address language questions directly, but he makes two important points about Davies and language, one of them in the concluding words of the book, in which, speaking of Davies's "essentially religious and moral" commitment to the self, he says:

> That such commitment is selfish, undemocratic, and elitist does not bother Robertson Davies in the least. Indeed, that commit-

ment, which is *typically expressed in the form of didactic pronouncements*, is the primary characteristic of his work as a whole.
(159)

The proposition italicized above (italics mine), though embedded and offered *en passant*, is essential to grasping Davies's style. Earlier in the book, Peterman makes another telling observation in his assessment of *The Manticore*:

> A heavily didactic novel, *The Manticore* is a falling off from the achievement of *Fifth Business*. It suffers by comparison in several ways. In the first place *there is little effective distinction between Ramsay's and David's voices. Though both books are told in the first-person and the two narrators are a generation apart, they share a sameness of voice and tone that is disconcerting.* (135, italics mine).

The same could be said moving back from *Fifth Business* to *A Voice from the Attic* or forward to *One Half of Robertson Davies*. Even though the books are presented as coming from three very different personae, the styles are astonishingly similar.

Stephen Bonnycastle's exploration of the ethics of monologue in Davies contains the most thorough and probing analysis yet both of the subject and of the uses of language in Davies. In working his way to the conclusion that Davies's "attempt to glorify [monologue], by exalting it above dialogue, is mistaken," he points repeatedly to the centrality of language and of the use of language in *Fifth Business* and *The Manticore*. Bonnycastle notes that in these two books real power is power of speech. The struggles in the books are verbal, and the winner of any struggle — in other words, the person who gets to attain, in Davies's view, "the summit of human discourse" by being the one who may engage in monologue — is always the one whose "vocabulary and power of analysis are stronger." The educative process for David Staunton is a matter of "learning and unlearning vocabulary" — of going from the language of his father to the language of Pargetter to the language of the psychiatrist Dr. Von Haller. Finally, the book "concludes . . . with David's promotion to a more powerful teacher, Liesl," who "belittles the psychiatrist and prepares David for a new language and a new range of experience." The choice between monologue and dialogue is "a choice between having an audience and having a partner," and in that choice not only Davies himself but his characters seem to prefer the hierarchical arrangement of monologist-audience to the equality of a genuine conversational partnership.

A synthesis of these critics would give us a stylistic portrait of a few brief, bold strokes. Those strokes seem to me not only brief and bold but accurate and telling. Davies's world is an hierarchical world in which language and its uses are central and are always conflated with questions of belief and of value. The lexis of money (*false* value) that permeates the world of Boy Staunton also pervades the early and unenlightened Dunny Ramsay and David Staunton's descriptions of his boyhood life. The lexis of awe (*true* value) attaches to Father Blazon and to Liesl and, to a somewhat lesser extent, to Dr. Von Haller. The instruction given the reader by implication through such verbal collocation is reinforced by pontifical pronouncement from the mouths of authority figures in the books (Father Blazon, Dr. Von Haller, Liesl): maxim and generalization in the didactic mode are frequent, and — to use the terms of classical rhetoric — the Topos of Authority[2] is more common in Davies than in most other 20th-century writers.

To the portrait above, I would add some notions from my own stylistic research. Given the ethical and ideological assumptions, we might well expect Davies to look for his paradigms of language in times and places remote from late 20th-century North America. He does not disappoint us: his normal idiom is British English, specifically British English of the literate class between the time of Fielding and the time of Thackeray. Before starting the figure-and-text anatomy of Davies's syntax I should note that I could find little to correct in the received descriptions of his views and his use of language.[3] What follows here is an elaboration of the brief but astute observations made by my most able predecessors. The samples to be used for this analysis are given in Table 5.1.

TABLE 5.1

Samples Used for Chapter 5

NONFICTION	FICTION
Davies, *Voice from the Attic*	Davies, *Fifth Business*
Layton, *Engagements*	Davies, *The Manticore*
Woodcock, *Rejection of Politics*	MacLennan, *Two Solitudes*
Frye, *Fables of Identity*	Buckler, *The Mountain and The Valley*
Richler, *Hunting Tigers*	Richler, *Duddy Kravitz*
Dobbs, *Reading the Time*	Wiseman, *The Sacrifice*
Atwood, *Survival*	Callaghan, *Native Argosy/Strange Fugitive*
Conrad, *Prefaces*	Atwood, *The Edible Woman*
Orwell, *Collected Essays*	Conrad, *The Secret Agent*
Callaghan, *That Summer in Paris*	Orwell, *1984*
	James, *Washington Square*

Richler, Atwood, and Callaghan were chosen because they are the Canadian writers in this book other than Davies who are scrutinized in both nonfiction and fiction. Similarly Orwell and Conrad, who together provide some "British" benchmarks: like Davies, they were born outside of the U.K. and were introduced to the very best kind of English as aliens. The remaining controls, except James, were chosen for proximity of birth year. And James himself was picked as another North American of aristocratic inclination who deliberately sought models and methods in the language and customs of places far distant from his native turf.

Sentences & Clauses

The Davies sentence, though tidy, is somewhat long in relation to both time and genre (Figure 5.1). His independent clauses are more numerous in nonfiction than the mean for the controls, less numerous than the mean in fiction (Figure 5.2). Similarly, his ratio of rankshifted clauses to independent is below the mean in nonfiction, above the mean in fiction (Figure 5.3). In both these measures for these three books, Davies's practice is stable from genre to genre, just as it is in the additioning of clauses: we can expect a coordinator-additioned independent clause to an average density of one every 80 words, one every 2.6 sentences (Figure 5.4). Consider two characteristic utterances (additioning coordinators underlined):

> Much that is badly written and grossly padded must be read rapidly *and* nothing is lost thereby. (*Vox* 10)

> Dickens' Dr. Blimber was one kind of Victorian schoolmaster, *and* Mr. Curdle, who defined the dramatic unities as "a kind of universal dove-tailedness with regard to place and time," typifies Dr. Blimber's duller pupils. (*Vox* 25)

The two sentences, 17 and 34 words respectively, suggest the range of his preferred length as well as the mean (22.4 to 27.5 words per sentence over the three samples, with the mean 25.5). More importantly, they illustrate his strong affection for the compound-complex sentence and his preference within the rankshifted clauses for those that are finite (first sentence, *that*; second sentence, *who*) — i.e. for the relative and the subordinate clauses as opposed to the nonfinite, whose rankshift is carried by a verbal.

Coordinator-additioning is not his only habitual way of seriating clauses; many of his sentences have internal full stops (Figure 5.5), a device in which he ranks above the mean for the controls in both genres. We should not be surprised to encounter, from time to time, sentences like the following:

> The scene is one of bustling domesticity: your wife is writing to her mother, on the typewriter, and from time to time she appeals to you for the spelling of a word; the older children are chattering happily over a game, and the baby is building, and toppling, towers of blocks. (*Vox* 10–11)

Similarly, speaking in the voice of Dunny Ramsay, he writes:

> Rehearsal was difficult because much depended on the girls who collected the objects; they had to use their heads, and their heads were not the best-developed part of them. (*Fifth* 213)

The six-clause compound sentence simply illustrates his propensity for compounding at its most inflamed; it has two internal full stops — a colon and a semi-colon. The compound-complex sentence in Ramsay's voice, linked by a semi-colon, is more typical of Davies's usual practice.

His strong tendency to use finite rankshifted clauses is illustrated by Figures 5.6 and 5.7: this is, of course, the reverse of the modern

practice of preferring the nonfinites, and the antiquity of the resonances set off by such a preference is sometimes underscored by the
old-fashioned trick of left-branching the sentence opening:

> *When* she was twelve, though, she was sure *that* she was going
> to be another Myra Hess and worked very hard. (*Man* 129)

> *Although* I cannot vouch for this, I have always thought it
> suspicious *that* Leola opened her windows one afternoon, *when*
> the nurse had closed them, and took a chill, and was dead in less
> than a week. (*Fifth* 193)

Notice the explicitness with which the rankshifted clauses are subordinated (no locutions like "she was sure // she was . . ." or "it is
suspicious // Leola opened . . .").

The compound sentence, though in the language from time indeterminate, is essentially a device of the 18th century; it was then that
its use reached its peak for the Modern English Period. It remained
strong well into the 1800s — an instrument of frequent recourse not
only for Scott and Austen but for writers as late as Trollope, Morris,
and Newman. In our century, the age of Orwell, Will Strunk, and
Mies van der Rohe, it has gone out of style, as we have already seen
in chapter 2. Its use in Davies does more than give him a balanced and
stately sentence frame; together with other elements in the style, it
makes suggestions about time and place to which we shall return later
in this chapter.

Predication

Earlier in the book, I called Davies's style "static" — i.e. non-active
and dealing with states. His preferences in predication (Figure 5.8) are
indicative: he has fewer active predicators than any of the controls
except Conrad in nonfiction. On the fiction side, he has fewer than
any of the six Canadians and exceeds only three of the controls — the
Victorians James and Conrad, and George Orwell, whose principal,
Winston Smith, *does* little though much *is done* unto him.

The flip side of Figure 5.8 is Figure 5.9 — the finite *be* forms, copula
and passive; he likes to tell us how it *is*, or how it should *be done*
among the clerisy or the inner circle or the better sort. Notice that in
both these figures the total opposition with Callaghan to which we

referred in the opening paragraph of the chapter is strongly highlighted. Davies's affection for *be*-form predicators produces considerable complementation in his prose (Figure 5.10), and these two features combine with his suppression of the active voice to produce echoes of another great pontificator and man of letters, Samuel Johnson. Indeed, Johnson's definition of Natural Law might well have been Davies's ("Natural Law *is* that which *is* always and everywhere true about the better sort of people.").

Important also are the things that Davies tends to avoid: not just the active voice and the tiresome, declassé expense of energy that it suggests, but also two essentially Germanic verb forms. Participles and progressives (ongoing aspect), both of them *ing* forms, are illustrated in Figure 5.11; postpositions are illustrated in Figure 5.12. Both such forms are inescapable in English, but it is clear that Davies tends to avoid them more than the rest of us. In Davies's prose, "we have fed on the dainties that are bred in a book; we have eat paper and drunk ink; our intellect is replenished" (*Vox* 39). But we will not "see Irwin *sitting up* in bed with the flashlight" (Richler, *Duddy Kravitz* 69).

Simply isolating the finite predicators from the illustrative text offered thus far in this chapter is an instructive exercise (*be* predicators marked 213, passives marked 022):

is   (213)
have been made   (022)
have failed
is badly written   (022)
(is) grossly padded   (022)
is lost   (022)
was   (213)
defined
typifies
is   (213)
is writing
appeals
are chattering
is building
(is) toppling
was   (213)
depended
collected

had to use
were not   (213)
was   (213)
was going to be   (213)
worked
cannot vouch
thought
opened
had closed
took
was   (213)
have fed
are bred   (022)
(have drunk)
is replenished   (022)

The six-clause compound sentence of page 102 slightly skews this set of examples with the four ongoing-aspect (progressive) verb phrases. But the density of *be* heads and of passives is indicative, as is the density of perfective tense forms, which, at 17% of the total, again harkens back to an earlier time (*vide* Chapter 2). The density of *be* heads has a concomitant in Davies's love of complementation (Figure 5.10).

Noun Phrases

We have already noted in Chapter 2 the nominal upcreep of the last 180 years: from the time of Jane Austen to the 1970s, the norm for noun density in literary nonfiction prose rose from 20% of text to 25% — one of the most massive changes in the Modern English Period. Figure 5.13 suggests that it is a trend from which Davies holds himself aloof — unlike Orwell, Richler, Woodcock, and others. Davies's figure of 22.1% nouns in a nonfiction work sits on the mean for the middle of the 19th century. These (fewer) nouns are likelier than in other writers to be preceded by an indefinite determiner (a/an/any — Figure 5.14), and the resonant echoes produced by this tendency — in combination with his many *be* forms — are not those of W.C. Fields ("*A* man who hates children and dogs can't *be* all bad");

they are yet another Johnsonian element in Davies's nonfiction style ("*A* man who *is* tired of London *is* tired of life"). In Davies's own words:

> *Any* book *is a* good book which feeds the mind something which may enlarge it, or move it to action. *A* book *is* good in relation to its reader. (*Vox* 293)

As we might expect, he avoids the attributive noun. Indeed, he may be more scrupulously reticent with this usage than any other living writer in the language (Figure 5.15). Consider the following passage from *The Manticore*, together with some possible options for the noun phrases therein:

<table>
<tr><td>**DAVIES**</td><td>**OPTION**</td></tr>
<tr><td>This was important to me because another kind of art was coming to the fore at home. Caroline, who had always had lessons on the piano, was beginning to show some talent as a musician.
(*Man* 129)</td><td>This was important to me because another *art form* was showing up on the *home front*. Caroline, who had always had *piano lessons,* was beginning to show some musical talent.</td></tr>
</table>

It is not only attributive modification that Davies avoids. He also tends not to use either apposition (with nouns) or postmodification (with adjectives) — Figure 5.17. But he does qualify his nouns extensively, with both prepositional phrase and relative clause. Figure 5.18 shows Davies's preposition-to-noun ratio in relation to those of the controls: he is above the mean in this usage and above most of the controls, as many of the things that pop up as attributives in other prose writers occur as prepositional phrases in this writer of prose. Figure 5.19 shows his use of the (qualifying) restrictive relative clause — to a level that again is well over a century behind present-day norms. Dunny Ramsay can illustrate the uses of both of these qualifiers (noun-modifying prepositional phrases and restrictive relative clauses in italic):

> So he made some shrewd short-term investments *in the stock market* and was thus able to live at a rate *that puzzled and annoyed the old man,* who waited angrily for him to get into debt. (*Fifth* 113)

For I was, as you may have already guessed, a collaborator *with Destiny*, not one *who put a pistol to its head and demanded particular treasures*. (*Fifth* 169)

The Davies noun phrase, in addition to being fairly distinctive, builds a lot of retrospection into its structure. His relatively low density of nominals and his way of handling their modification look back to a time well over a century ago; they may also look to a different place, to different social mores, to different views on class from those that most Canadians today would acknowledge as theirs. Of these subjects, too, more later.

Other Word Class Usages

Figures 5.20 and 5.21 offer the numbers for total modifiers and for intensifiers in the Davies samples and the control samples. Both figures suggest that Davies exploits the adjective-adverb group with restraint in both genres, a fact that contributes to the impression of tidiness that I spoke of earlier in the chapter. Though a practiced stage-manager and a scrupulously calculating manager of the effects of his prose and of his persona, Davies to his credit never attempts to over-manage his language.

Both in total lexemes (Figure 5.22) and in lexemes plus pronouns (Figure 5.23) Davies ranks near the low end of the scale. A style so low in nominality and so relatively high in some of the more important function words (subordinators, relatives, prepositions) is inevitably going to be on the lower part of the scale in both these measures.

Davies vs. Davies

Peterman taxes Davies with failure to distinguish the voices of Dunny Ramsay and David Staunton. Indeed, in many measures Davies, Dunny, and David are all the same writer. A retrospective look at twelve of the figures in the chapter will suggest the degree of sameness. In period length (5.1), independent clause total (5.2), additioning of clauses (5.4), finite rankshifted clauses (5.6), non-complex sentences

(5.7), *ing*-forms (5.11), postpositions (5.22), attributive nouns (5.15), 31-01-01 (5.16), appositions and postmodifiers (5.17), restrictive relatives (5.19), and "M" (5.20) there is very little movement from work to work. Though there is some effect of genre in Davies — the fiction works are somewhat less static and more active in their predicators — the stability is remarkable by comparison with the genre-to-genre movement in the measures of the other writers. In these three books — all of them — the writer is Davies and genre be damned.

CONCLUSIONS

This is one of the great styles in 20th-century English prose: as tidy and as trenchant at times as Jack Granatstein's, as rich in myth, both local and universal, as that of Donald Creighton. It is wholly distinctive, and as out of joint with its time and its place as Carlyle's was. In such a case the critic must ask, what is the political and social "content" of this style: not just what does Davies write about (though this is surely part of it), but what meanings are embedded in the forms themselves?

Carlyle's style represented a highly conscious attempt to deFrancify English and bend the language back to a more Germanic mode — in short to turn away from the "vapouring, vainglorious, gesticulating" French in favour of the "noble, patient, pious" Germans.[4] He no doubt thought that a more Aryan, more Germanic English would be a more fertile linguistic medium from which heroes like Jocelyn of Brakelond might arise to lead the English back out of the wreckage of the industrial age.[5] The "content" of Carlyle's forms was racial, temporal, geographic, and political.

Davies has inverted the Carlylean process, rejecting the Germanic trends in literary English that have dominated the stylistic history of the last 160 years. Davies's syntax has strong affinities with the norms for mid-19th century English; his lexis, too, is often both temporally conservative and British in its resonances. Not many of our contemporaries are likely to use a vocabulary that includes a high density of old-fashioned items like *emulation, hortatory, base passions, folly, good taste, decent,* and *beldam.* Such tokens from our past are mixed into a lexical assortment that habitually includes heavy components of both social rank and religion (*grandee, noble, high priest, gentle birth*, and the like), to which are added sprinklings of Anglicisms (*boss*, where most of us would say employer; *did not play games* instead of our customary terms for athletic participation). The old Arnoldian questions of who's number one and who's number two are always present in his social observations, and even appear sometimes in his treatments of literature, as when he speaks of "the artist's superiority to mere outward rank" (*Vox* 192).

A man of Davies's education and intelligence does not come to such habitual syntax and lexis by way of Freudian slippage. He could not be unaware of the implications of his habitual patterns of choice. Study of the classical and Romance languages — especially of Latin and French — was at the heart of the humanist curriculum that educated the better sort of Englishman from the early 1500s until well into this century, and Latin and French provided the models for the English of Sidney, Milton, Dryden, Addison, Johnson, and even Arnold. To prefer these writers and their linguistic models to the German models that have guided our social scientists (Hegel, Marx, Freud, Marcuse, Weber, Durkheim) is to imply a cultural as well as a temporal judgement. It is with Johnson and Arnold that Davies has some of his strongest affinities — with Johnson for speaking in general about the human condition in frequently aphoristic form, with Arnold for the interest.in culture, for the insistent reliance on the Topos of Authority, and for the argumentation by personal view stated as immutable law.

The overall effect of monologues delivered in a style with such Johnsonian and Arnoldian elements in it is sometimes Olympian, sometimes pontifical, occasionally no more than pompous. What we are confronted with in these first-person texts is a writer who in several ways is convinced that he is far far better than the bulk of his fellow members of the human race. This is true not only of Davies but of his two *alter egos* Dunny and David. That superiority to the general run of the rest of us, based on superior "vocabulary and power of analysis," is often reinforced first by allusions and second by settings that are for the few and for the very few: Dame Myra Hess, the Uffizi, Goldsmith, Jung, Benjamin Britten, *Love's Labour's Lost*, Charles Lever among the allusions; Oxford, the Royal Alex, Rosedale, the headquarters of the Bollandists, and a thinly disguised Upper Canada College among the settings.

Style is no stranger to politics. The plainness of the early Puritans, the ostentatious asceticism of Ralph Nader, the long hair and tie-dyed uniforms of The Woodstock Nation, the inchoate, tetragram-saturated haranguing style of Mario Savio during the mid-60s in Berkeley, even the style of Alex Portnoy — all of these have been freighted not only with cultural resonances but with political intent and political objectives as well. And Davies, too, with wholly different objectives from any of the foregoing, turns to England and to an earlier time with political, as well as other, ends in view. In short, the "content" of Davies's forms is racial, temporal, geographic, and political, and I suspect that he is as well acquainted with this fact as any of his readers.

NOTES

1. Short titles in citations for the three Davies books used in this chapter are *Vox* for *Voice from the Attic*, *Fifth*, for *Fifth Business*, and *Man* for *Manticore*. The editions used are, respectively, the 1972 McClelland and Stewart paperback for *Vox*, the 1977 Penguin paperback for *Fifth*, and the 1972 Macmillan hardcover for *Man*.

2. To the four *topoi* of Aristotle (degree, possibility, past and future, and size) the Romans added classification, comparison, causation, and evidence, of which *authority* was a subcategory. Though primarily a *topos* for forensic discourse, authority was also considered useful for didactic purposes — those to which Davies insistently puts it.

3. Barbara Godard might seem at first to be an exception to this, but I think she is not. Godard takes issue with my view of Davies as a linguistic conservative, stating that Davies "has followed the model of the earlier Renaissance . . . in a dialectical process that simultaneously valorizes and derides both language worlds" (the ancient and the modern). The difference that I would see between my view of Davies and Godard's lies in differing views of the term *style*, which in her vocabulary seems to denote a far more conscious process than in mine. I have no doubt that a central tension in Davies's art is in the interface between the old and the new, and no doubt that Davies, like other great artists before him, is capable of briefly standing outside the prison of his style in order to mock the bars of his cage. Once beyond definitions, I can see no consequential differences in our respective views of Davies.

4. The phrases are from a letter that Carlyle wrote to *The Times* during the German annexation of Alsace-Lorraine in 1871. British opinion at the time was firmly pro-French.

5. Jocelyn of Brakelond, an 11th-century monk and superior of a monastery, was the Carlylean hero-figure of *Past and Present*, which Carlyle had turned to when his attempted biography of Cromwell proved intractable.

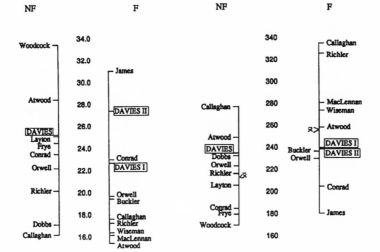

FIGURE 5.1
Average Period Length

FIGURE 5.2
Independent Clauses per Sample

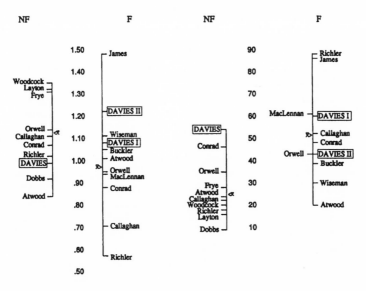

FIGURE 5.3
Rankshifted Clauses per
Independent Clause

FIGURE 5.4
And/or — *Added Independent*
Clauses per Sample

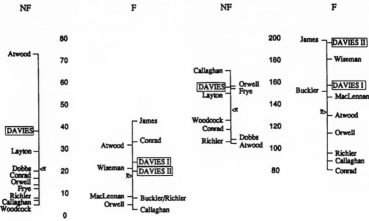

FIGURE 5.5
*Intrasentence Full Stops
per Sample (98)*

FIGURE 5.6
*Finite Rankshifted Clauses
per Sample (42 + 43 + 00)*

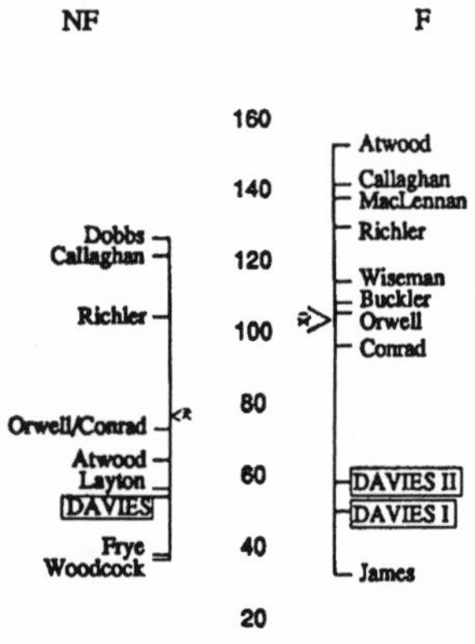

FIGURE 5.7
*Periods per Sample with no
Subordinator (42) or Relative (43)*

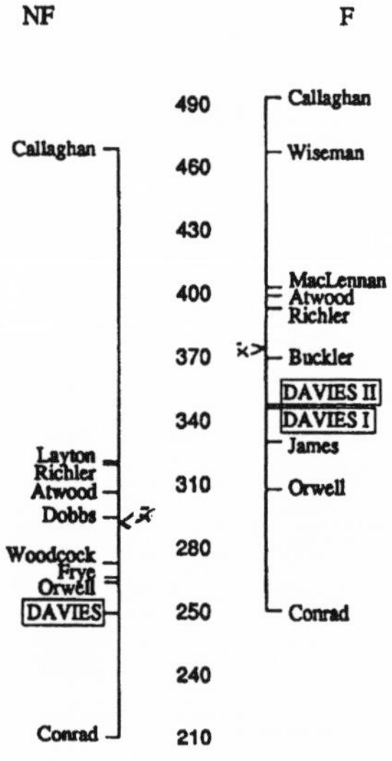

FIGURE 5.8
*Active Constructions
(Nonfinites included)*

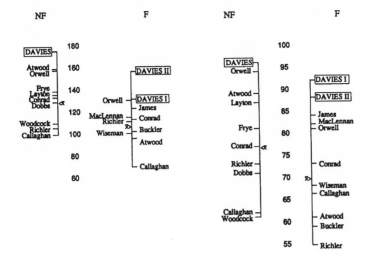

FIGURE 5.9
Finite be *plus Passive Transitives (213 + 022)*

FIGURE 5.10
Complementation : Predicate Adjectives (032) + Predicate Nouns (014)

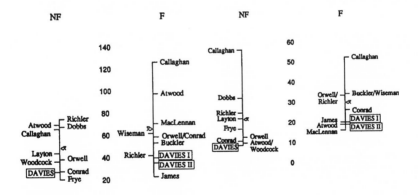

FIGURE 5.11
Dutchmen : ing *Verb Forms (023 + 06)*

FIGURE 5.12
Dutchmen : Postpositions (32)

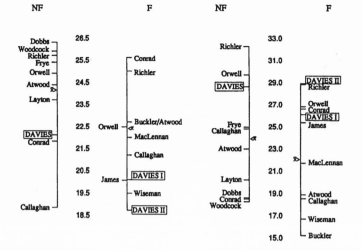

FIGURE 5.13
Nouns as % (01)

FIGURE 5.14
*Indefinite Determiners as % of
all Determiners (313/31)*

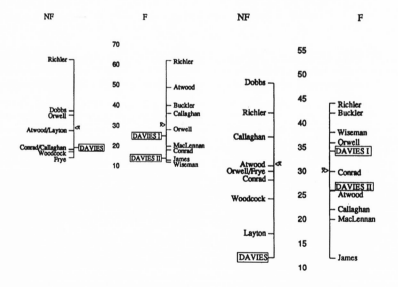

FIGURE 5.15
Dutchmen : Attributive Nouns (012)

FIGURE 5.16
*Determiner – Noun – Noun
(31-01-01)*

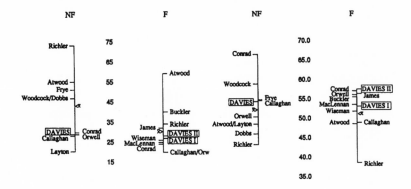

FIGURE 5.17
Postmodifying Adjectives (035)
+ Appositives (017)

FIGURE 5.18
Prepositions as % of Nouns (51/01)

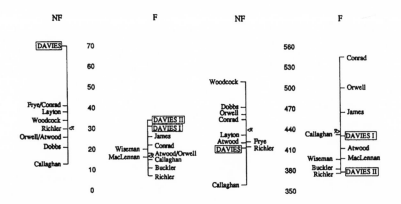

FIGURE 5.19
Restrictive Relatives (433)

FIGURE 5.20
"M" Statistic
(03 + 04 + 33 + 34)

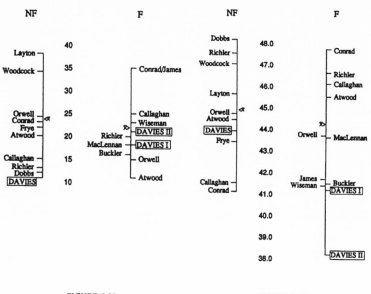

FIGURE 5.21
Intensifiers (33)

FIGURE 5.22
Lexemes as %
(01 + 02 + 03 + 04 + 05 + 06 + 07)

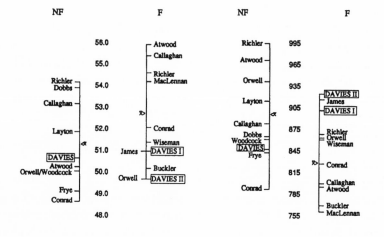

FIGURE 5.23
Lexemes + Pronouns (11) as %

FIGURE 5.24
"D" Statistic

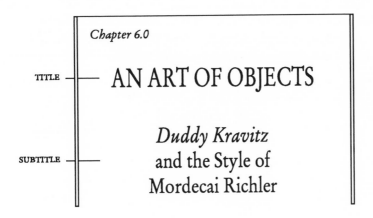

TITLE ——— AN ART OF OBJECTS

SUBTITLE ——— *Duddy Kravitz*
and the Style of
Mordecai Richler

From the first day, Mordecai Richler's career as an artist has shown a central interest in questions of style. Indeed, his first book, *The Acrobats*, has affinities — parabolic though strong — with Raymond Queneau's *Exercises in Style*, and his subsequent works show an unerring eye and ear for elements of constant form — both style in language and style in life. The life-style and thinking style of upper middle class liberals and Hampstead (*Cocksure* and *SUH*), the WASP style of Mortimer Griffin and the abrasive Jewish style of Ziggy Spicehandler (*Cocksure*), the verbal style of Mrs. Jacobs, heiress to the mantle of legendary Jenny Grossinger of the Big G (*Hunting Tigers*) — these all etch themselves in acid in the mind of anyone who reads those books. Richler, like the other three Canadians in the adjacent chapters of this book, is pre-eminently a style-conscious writer.

As in the case of Davies, the critics have elected to acknowledge this centre of consciousness *en passant* rather than grappling with it directly. Nevertheless, over the years they have managed to fasten several words on the phenomenon of Richler's style: *satiric* (embraced by all of his critics as well as by Richler himself[1]); *cinematic* and *cinematographic* (Woodcock [*Richler*] probably first and after him everyone else); *fragmented/fragmentation*, together with their cousins *disjunct* and *asymmetrical* (Bonnycastle ["Structure"] in the first instance, myself in the second); an art of *collocation* that focuses on *cliché* (Michael Greenstein); and finally an art essentially of *moral seriousness* (Wilfred Cude and Derek Cohen pre-eminently). To none of these visions of Richler's style is there any dissent except the last. The dissenters in this case tend to suggest that because Richler has no positive program, because he only points to negative things, he is not a genuine moralist.[2] On this question I personally am with Cude and Cohen, but that really does not matter: the question generates enough discussion to suggest that, positively or negatively, moral questions are in there somewhere.

Of all the critics to treat Richler, the one to deal most directly with style has been Michael Greenstein. He concentrates on the pervasive lexis of hurry, particularly various forms of the verb *run*, and on the element of cliché in Richler's art. But Greenstein's excellent study and my own previous consideration of the syntax of *Duddy Kravitz* alone are the only things to date that deal with what we are calling style in this book. So that the critical commentary on the style of Richler is much like the critical commentary on Davies's style — interesting and insightful pieces, but small pieces and scattered here and there.

It may be that the critical community has underestimated the degree to which a writer's art is rooted in language, the degree to which in a good book theme and structure reassert themselves in the sentence-by-sentence — even the phrase-by-phrase — process of composition. Various levels of language in a first class work of art tend to work together. In this regard, *Duddy Kravitz* is a book in which the syntactic skeptic or grammatical neophyte might well serve an apprenticeship. We shall have two objects here — direct and indirect — the style of the book and the style of Richler. It is with the former that we shall begin.

The Apprenticeship of Duddy Kravitz is one of two Richler novels in which the mainspring of the action is the reification or literalization of a cliché: "A man without land is nobody," says the old *zeyda*, and his bromide becomes Duddy's ruling passion, given a more-than-merely-verbal reality at the end of the book in Duddy's lake.[3] Decorum alone would dictate that reification should be so central; Richler's art is, after all, an art of objects — pop art at times — an art like that of many other satirists that traffics in the juxtaposition and *collocation* of things and phrases and words rather than in the *specification* of relations.[4] And that art asserts itself at every level of the text, especially at those we shall deal with here, syntax and lexis. We shall proceed as in previous chapters, comparatively, using controls from other Canadian fiction samples in the inventory. The samples to be used in this analysis are listed in Table 6.1.

TABLE 6.1

Samples Used for Chapter 6

Cohen, *The Favourite Game*	Ostenso, *Wild Geese*
Davies, *Fifth Business*	Atwood, *The Edible Woman*
Hood, *The Swing in the Garden*	de la Roche, *Jalna*
MacLennan, *Two Solitudes*	Laurence, *The Stone Angel*
Grove, *Fruits of the Earth*	Richler, *Duddy Kravitz*
Callaghan, *Strange Fugitive/Native Argosy*	

Sentences & Clauses

The *Duddy Kravitz* sentence is of middling length (Figure 6.1), showing a strong thrust towards parataxis. Although, as we shall see later, the book's density of finite predicators is normal for this group (Figure 6.9), its distribution of those predicators is skewed very strongly in a paratactic direction. *DK* is at the very bottom of the group in total rankshifted clauses and close to the bottom in finite rankshifted clauses (Figures 6.2 and 6.3). But it is in the upper end of the range in both sentences without dependent clauses (Figure 6.4) and total independent clauses (Figure 6.5). And its total of added clauses is higher than for any other text among those selected for this book (Figure 6.6). A look at one passage from our sample is revealing (Markings: *rs* = rankshifted clause; // = coordinated independent clause):

> Duddy was seven at the time // and a year earlier his mother had enrolled him in the Talmud Torah parochial school. Uncle Benjy was going through his Zionist phase at the time, // and he paid the tuition. Uncle Benjy also knew (rs) that his father, (rs) whom he hardly ever saw these days, walked hand in hand with Duddy

on St Dominique Street. But the round-shouldered men did not wonder // or turn away (rs) when they saw Simcha (rs) walking with his grandson. The old man had no more enemies // — even Katansky pitied him. The round-shouldered old men looked at Duddy // and decided (rs) he was mean, a crafty boy, // and they hoped (rs) he would not hurt Simcha too hard. (48)

This is an extraordinary array even for *Duddy Kravitz*: six compound sentences in a row, a total of thirteen independent clauses, within which there occur but six rankshifted clauses. Remarkable as it is, it is not an egregious caricature of the averages for the sample: 1.8 independent clauses per period, one rankshifted clause for every two independent.

The density of added clauses in combination with the suppression of dependencies gives this text a uniquely paratactic character. The parataxis is fashioned to satiric ends. A particularly good example comes from our introduction to Peter John Friar (Markings: // = coordinated independent clauses):

It had been shown at the Edinburgh Festival // and had won a prize in Turkey, // but even though he had directed it his name was not actually on the picture for a dark reason he only hinted at. (114)

The double-barrelled bathos, first of winning a prize in Turkey and then of Friar's name not being on the film, is laid out plainly — in a parallel series. The total density of word-parallelism (Figure 6.7) is only one more reflection of the generally additive and serial kind of art of which we have been speaking from the beginning. Things are not just added; they are added up (Figure 6.8).

Phrases – Verbs

Richler is a copious generator of independent clauses, and this in turn makes him relatively copious in the generation of finite clauses of all kinds. Each of the finite verb phrases in Figure 6.9 marks a finite clause; *DK*, though the *median* text of the group, sits some 5% above the *mean*, and this despite Richler's tendency to avoid dependent clauses of all kinds.

Those verb phrases have a distinction of their own. They are unlikely to contain auxiliaries of any kind, but especially unlikely to contain tense auxiliaries (do/did, will/would, have/ had). Richler's preference is strongly for the simple unspecified past (markings: *verbs* in italic):

> Crossing the tracks they *came* out on a rocky slope on the edge of the mountain. The dew soon *soaked* through Duddy's shoes and trouser bottoms. His body *ached*. The excitement of the game and search past, he *longed* for his bed, but Yvette *led* him deeper into the field. (92)

The preference is borne out by Figure 6.10 (Tense Auxiliaries). The verb phrase heads are usually bare, and contributing to their bareness is Richler's strong tendency to avoid the verb-modifying words — adverbs and function adverbs. Of our group he is the most sparing user of the latter (Figure 6.11), and is among the most sparing of adverbs in general (Figure 6.12). The tendency to avoid the adverb is an aspect of his being a sparse user of all the modifying words — adjectives, adverbs, intensifiers, and function adverbs (Figure 6.13).

A final aspect of the verb phrases of *Duddy Kravitz* is the fairly frequent recourse to postposition verbs (Figure 6.14: "Yvette did *up* the top button of his coat . . ." [206]). Though its frequency in this text does not reach the heights established by the works of Callaghan and Laurence, it is still 25% above the mean for this group.

Phrases – Nouns

The trimming of the size of the verb phrase and the suppression of modifiers leaves Richler lots of room for deployment of his more favoured items: numbers (Figure 6.8), nouns (Figure 6.15), and pronouns. Richler is a highly nominal writer, and his total for nouns and pronouns together is capped only by Hood (Figure 6.17). Many of these nouns register as lacking attributive modification of any kind (Figure 6.16) because Richler likes to refer to his characters by name: in one two-page sequence he refers to Duddy by name fourteen times and to other characters by name a total of fifteen times (87-88). He tends to avoid the relative clause (Figure 6.18).

However, once the proper names are cranked out, and they make up a large proportion of Figures 6.15 and 6.16, we can get to Richler's true love: the packed noun phrase. Determiners and adjectives he can almost do without (Figures 6.21 and 6.22), since what a noun phrase needs is clearly more nouns. Richler is very free with attributive nouns, nouns used in the customary adjective position and function, and it is not just the *recreation hall* or the *kitchen sink* or the *stick boy*; it is also *The Talmud Torah Elementary School, stamp business profits,* and the *high score competition.* A measure of his penchant for this kind of noun phrase building is given in Figure 6.20 (Attributive Nouns). To the right of the phrase head, Richler is apt to add more material — especially appositions and postmodifying adjectives. Figure 6.23 suggests the density of all this front-and-back packing material. Here are some typically Richlerian nominal phrases:

Nobody, not even Katansky . . . (47)

The officer in charge of Duddy's neighbourhood — tubby, middle-aged Benny Feinberg . . . (52)

The company, one of many . . . (55)

One of Duddy's comic book suppliers, a Park Avenue newsstand proprietor named Barney . . . (55)

a sixteen page comic-book-like production titled *Dick Tracy's Night Out* . . . (55)

The drawings, crude black and white . . . (55)

Dick Tracy, sporting an enormous erection with the words 'drip, drip, drip' and an arrow pointing to it from underneath . . . (55)

The packed noun phrase gives Richler a fine vehicle for his favourite satirical technique after reification — the preposterous collocation. In the phrases listed above, there are several comic resonances set off simply by proximity: Nobody-Katansky; Park Avenue-newsstand-Barney; officer-in-charge — tubby, middle-aged; and finally the very obvious collocations in the Tracy piece. He can use his penchant for seriation, especially noun phrase seriation, in the same way:

. . . three Protestant schools, two parochials, the Bnai Brith Youth House, a yeshiva, and at least four poolrooms and a bowling alley. (56)

The prepositional phrase that consists of preposition-determiner-noun (51-31-01) tends insistently to be the most common three-class sequence in English. Only in the work of exceptionally heavy-handed modifying writers like Walter Pater, Charles Reich, and Lewis Mumford does the pattern get eclipsed by another (in their cases, determiner-adjective-noun: 31-03-01). In *Duddy Kravitz*, the prepositional phrase is indeed the most common three-class pattern, but it occurs far less often than in any of the control authors except for two linguistic ascetics, Laurence and Atwood (Figure 6.25). Figures 6.24 and 6.25 suggest just how sparing he is of prepositional constructions: the three-word prepositional phrase is, with noun-coordinator-noun, one of the two most common period endings in the language, terminating on the average one sentence in six; in Richler, its density is roughly half that. And among our eleven writers, he alone is a deviant from one of the great rules of proportion of literary English: one preposition for every two nouns.

What animates this aversion is hard to say, but one suggestion has been made to us — namely, that Richler's Yiddish milieu fosters the habit of building noun phrases in the German style with attributive nouns, rather than in the French with postmodifying prepositional phrases. True perhaps, but probably not a full account of the prodigious and wholly eccentric suppression of prepositional devices that characterizes the language of this work.

Richler also suppresses the relative clause: the 16 relatives for the *Duddy Kravitz* sample are roughly half the mean for this group, less than a third of the *Fifth Business* sample. This may be an aspect of the generally informal character of Richler's writing (*My Uncle Harry Morton* is less formal than *Harry Morton, who is my uncle*). As such it joins with the postposition verb (*get up* less formal than *arise*) and the suppression of prepositional phrase (*table top* less formal than *top of the table*) to produce a style 180° opposite from the formal style of Davies. Richler's use of the language is not only informal, it embodies the apparent future direction of things as clearly and as assertively as that of Davies embodies the stylistic values of the age of Victoria.

In a style so suffused with parataxis and seriation, a style in which various forms of parallelism overwhelm other syntactic devices, we should expect a low index of variety of phrase structure. Asymmetrical writers tend to produce high "D" values (830 and up), symmetrical writers low "D" values (770 down to 450). There is also a correlation with period length: writers of long periods tend to have high "D"; those with short periods, low. Richler is in the paradoxical position of writing relatively short periods while having a very high "D" (Figure 6.26). In short, he is a *very* asymmetrical writer, even while employing many parallel forms — notably seriation and the compound sentence. But within those symmetrical forms — just as within his other juxtapositions and collocations — there is an irresistible tendency towards almost perversely skewed asymmetry. Consider the series quoted above (syntactic coding given in parentheses):

three Protestant schools (81-03-01)
two parochials (81-03)
the Bnai Brith Youth House (31-01-01-01)
a yeshiva (31-01)
and at least four poolrooms (41-34-81-01-01)
and a bowling alley (41-31-01-01)

It is a truly extraordinary series, in which the semantic disjunctions of the lexis are underlined by the asymmetry of the syntax.

LEXIS

Cliché

Two important properties of Richler as an artist are an eye and an ear for cliché, as we have noted in some of his works at the beginning of this chapter.

Clichés are important also in *Duddy Kravitz*, especially in the dialogue:

"You'll go far, Kravitz." (40)
"Have another on me." (114)
"you go right ahead." (114)
"this one's on me, old chap." (114)
"you're going too far this time." (203)
"I'm going to stick with you." (203)

"I'm wondering how long you can keep this up before you fall flat on your face." (204)

"Take it easy. . ." (204)

"Long time no see." (205)

"Necessity is the mother of all invention." (209)

"That's show biz." (209)

"it's time to forgive and forget." (230)

"Can't you let bygones be bygones?" (230)

"There's no love lost between us." (230)

Sometimes the clichés are skewed, as in Max's dictum, "The world is full of shits," the pluralization of the last word being, perhaps, an inadvertant irony on the part of Max. Usually, however, they are given to us straight, particularly when they are clichés about money. Consider the following (speaker's name inserted):

HERSH: "Writing isn't a career. It's a vocation. I'm not in it for the money." (223)

MAX(!): "Money is the root of all evil." (293)

DUDDY: "Man does not live by bread alone." (225)

DUDDY: "Money isn't everything, Mr. Cohen." (264)

The characters themselves seem to be as aware of cliché as the reader might be. When Duddy threw the book's central cliché at Jerry Dingleman ("A man without land is nobody"), "Dingleman grasped that the boy was repeating somebody else's platitude" (159).

A general observation to be made here is that the presence of cliché in Richler's writing is an almost certain sign of the presence of insincerity in the character(s) he is depicting. A further observation germane to the work at hand is that at no point in *Duddy Kravitz* does anyone utter the words "Money is Time," or "Time is Money," for cliché in Richler never speaketh true. As Hersh says to Duddy at their brief reunion, after Duddy speaks of Paris ("Boy, I understand that the dames there . . ."):

"That's a cliché. It isn't true." (223)

Time

Duddy's apprenticeship is a constant race *for* money *against* time. It is therefore natural that the lexis of time should also represent a dominant motif in the book. Throughout the book, time is carefully specified — days of the week, months, years, and the lexis of time is repeatedly collocated with money and success and with those who possess them. Note the conversation with Mr. Cohen (markings: *time* words in italic):

> "Cheers."
> "You want a helping hand? A loan *until* you get on your feet again?"
> "No. But thanks just the same."
> "Duddy," Mr. Cohen said sternly, "you won't find me plastered like this *again* in *another five years*. Take while I'm in an offering mood. I'm not the Red Cross that you can call at any emergency."
> "But I'm not sure what I want to do any more."
> "Well, whatever you want to do, don't stand under any faculty derricks for thirty-five bucks *a week*. That's how people get killed. *Good night* and good luck."
> *After* Duddy had gone Mr. Cohen took his drink into the kitchen and got some more ice.
> The *goy* had hollered, he had rolled his eyes, and it had taken him *longer than an hour* to die. The health inspector had cost him five hundred dollars, but the case had never come to court. Death by misadventure was how the coroner put it. And *five weeks later* the coroner had sent Mr. Cohen a Christmas card and, terrified, Mr. Cohen had phoned his lawyer.
> "Don't lose sleep," the lawyer said. "Send him a case of scotch. The best there is."
> Mr. Cohen *still* had the card. It was one of those religious ones, *Joyeux Noël* and a *Yoshka* on the cross. Some sense of humour they have, he thought. (266)

Central to this vocabulary is the word *time* itself. It has some incidental collocations. For example, Hugh Thomas Calder is written up in *Time*, and when Duddy gets his office he tells Yvette to buy *Fortune*, *Time*, and *Life*. But most of all the plain word *time* is collected with two of the book's dominant presences: Jerry Dingleman and Lac St. Pierre. Note when Yvette first shows Duddy the lake:

> She watched as he swam out and dived down to the bottom *time* after *time*. . . . Once more he plunged to the bottom, nearer the shore this *time*. . . .
> "But you've come here before?"

"Yes."

"Many *times?*" (98–99)

The word is similarly prominent in the scene where Duddy first meets Jerry Dingleman, The Boy Wonder (markings: *time* in italic):

There was the question of the girls in and out of his apartment three-four at a *time* . . . . Olive never stayed in Montreal for more than three weeks at a *time* . . . . It was Dingleman, they said, who got her out of Bellevue that *time.* (133–34)

The last *time* out Ike Williams had knocked him silly in three rounds . . . . From that *time* on he was fuzzy in the head and had to stay home . . . . But nobody ever got funny with him when the Boy Wonder was around and there were *times* when Shub got his own back too. (134–35)

After the attempted brushoff from Shub, Dingleman's bodyguard, is the offer of a busboy's job at the Tico-Tico:

"Look, you've got to start somewhere. If you're O.K. Charlie'll be giving you tables of your own in no *time*" (135)

And Dingleman himself dismisses Duddy:

"Another *time*, sonny." (136)

The book's last major scene brings together the two sides of Duddy on a knoll above Lac St. Pierre — the grasping, stop-at-nothing hustler in the person of Jerry Dingleman, and the genuinely though perversely devoted family-man in the person of old Simcha Kravitz, of whose words the land on which they stand is an incarnation. In an implicit acknowledgment of those two sides, Duddy speaks to each of the men. To Simcha:

"And *Zeyda*," Duddy said, "you just take your *time* and look around and pick a lot, any lot, and that's where I'll put up your private house." (307)

To Jerry:

"Last *time* I saw you," Duddy said, "you couldn't even raise three thousand dollars. Remember, sonny?" (310)

As it works towards its conclusion, the scene offers two further perspectives on *time*, the first from Max, ever-ready with a cliché and always wrong:

"Time heals." (313)

The second is from Yvette, to whom Richler rightly gives the final word on *time*. It is the last use of the word in the book:

"You can have all the *time* in the world, Duddy. But I don't ever want to see you again." (314)

Throughout, the word *time* is used in two senses: what the French would call *temps* and what they would call *fois*. It is with decency (Yvette) and family (Simcha) that *time-temps* tends to be collocated, with Jerry Dingleman that *time-fois* tends to be collocated. In the last major scene, these tendencies, as one might infer from the last four quotations, constitute a rule. A further set of strong collocates of *time-temps* lies in the lexis of *run-hurry-hustle* scrutinized by Greenstein.

Know and Understand

The mainspring of the plot of *Duddy Kravitz* is a misunderstanding: "A man without land is nobody" Duddy takes literally rather than as an expression of longing from a tired, city-bound old man. *Know* and *understand*, with all their shades of difference, are often collocated in the book, and they tend to be the terms in which Duddy's ties of love and affection are defined (markings: *Know* and *Understand* in *italic*):

Duddy found his grandfather seated next to the Quebec heater in the shoe repair shop. "I won't beat around the bush," Duddy said.

"Good."

"Maybe it's not in my place, *Zeyda*, but don't you think whatever it is you have against Uncle Benjy it's time to forgive and forget?"

"How can I go and see him now?"

"But you used to be so close. Can't you let bygones be bygones?"

"Your Uncle Benjy is no idiot, and he *knows* me very well. If I went to see him all of a sudden he'd *understand* right away why." Simcha put the kettle on top of the Quebec heater and brought the bottle out. "All I'd have to do is ring his bell and he'd *know* it was no ulcer."

"Does Auntie Ida *know*?"

"She's in New York."

"With the other man?"

Simcha nodded. "Somebody should tell her. She has a right to *know*."

"Yeah."

"Benjy can't even get into the States any more. They say he's a communist."

"Guess who goes? Shit."

Simcha served him tea and brandy. "You have to be very, very careful because if she does come back with you he mustn't suspect why. Your Uncle Benjy is a proud man."

"There's no love lost between us. You *know* that, I hope."

"You don't *understand* each other."

"I worked for him once," Duddy said.

"We're a small family, Duddele."

"I didn't say I wasn't going, did I? It's just that he'd do anything for Lennie and he's always made fun of me and my ambitions. I'm living with a *shiksa*," Duddy said.

"I *know*." (229–30)

By the end of the book, Duddy has finished his apprenticeship and *knows* how to grab the land surrounding Lac St. Pierre, but he cannot *understand* Simcha's ethical scruples or Yvette's pervasive decency. Once again, Yvette marks the final uses of the words in this motif, and paradoxically in the final exchanges it is she who speaks of knowing, Duddy who speaks of understanding (markings: *Know* and *Understand* in italic):

"I don't *know* what you are any more. I don't care, either."

"I had to act quickly, Yvette . . . . Don't you *understand*?" (314)

A little further, the motif finishes:

"I want you to *know* something. *I'd* sue you. I'd even get Irwin Shubert to take the case. But Virgil won't let me. He doesn't even want to hear about it any more."

"You hate me," Duddy said. "Is that possible?"

"I think you're rotten. I wish you were dead."

"You don't *understand*, Yvette. Why can't I make you *understand*?" (315)

Richler's art is an art of collocation, and thus it comes as no surprise to learn that in his aspiring-writer days he was reading Evelyn Waugh, one of the great satiric collocators of our time, for whom he has expressed great admiration.[5] The most insistent lexical manifestations in *The Apprenticeship of Duddy Kravitz* cannot be looked at for themselves alone; they must be considered as expressions of the major thematic substance of the book and in terms of their collocates. Cliché, money, time, and knowing *are* the substance of this book.

Of Kravitz-Style and Richler-Style

To what extent will the style of a single text delineate the style of the writer? It is a question often mooted in places where one finds those who are interested in style. The answer, if we can believe the overwhelming preponderance of scholarship in the writer-attribution field, is that the single text is *highly* indicative. The single text, however, is not infallible: it may contain elements atypical of the writer's *oeuvre* as a whole, or it may miss a few elements that are in the style of all the other works in that *oeuvre*.

Nearly all the elements that we have discovered in *Kravitz*-style are also to be found in a computer analysis of *Hunting Tigers under Glass*, and all of them, I should say, are susceptible of recognition in *Cocksure*. Without computer-sampling of a third Richler work, I would not stake my scholarly reputation on a definition of *Richler's* style. But I can point out which of the elements discussed in this chapter are present in *Hunting Tigers* and which not. The affinities are suggestive, if not conclusive.

The essentially paratactic thrust of Richler's art and of his uses of language is strongly visible in the other work, as we can see by reconsidering some of the Figures in previous chapters. His middling sentence length can be seen in Figures 3.6 and 5.1, the suppression of rankshifted clauses, especially of finite rankshifted clauses, in 3.2 and 5.6. Similarly, his above-average use of simple and compound (as opposed to complex) forms is visible in 3.7 and 5.7. In the nonfiction work he uses a different system of boundaries and the text shows a massive reduction from *DK* in the generation of added clauses (from 90 down to 18 — Figure 3.4). Otherwise the parataxis of *Duddy Kravitz* is an equally strong structural principle in *Hunting Tigers*.

In the building of the verb phrase, the suppression of tense auxiliaries visible in *DK* is also a constituent of *Hunting Tigers* (Appendix A); similarly, the suppression of the adverbial modifiers (Appendix A, Figure 3.18). The durability of his affection for Germanic verb forms — *ing*-forms and postposition verbs — can be seen in Figures 5.10 and 5.11.

The noun phrases that we have spoken of in this chapter are also pervasive in *Hunting Tigers*. The suppression of prepositions (Figure 5.18) and of relative clauses (3.12), and the frequent use not only of attributive nouns (5.15) but of other noun phrase packing devices (5.17) are characteristic of both texts. Richler's nominality (3.13, 5.13), together with his general density of the lexeme group (3.19, 5.22), is also strongly characteristic of both texts.

The high level of parallel seriation that we noted in *DK* carries over into the later book. Appendix A shows that, with 90 word seriations, the *Hunting Tigers* sample — of all the ones used in this book — has more word parallelism than any Canadian work written by a writer born since 1930 except *Shrug*. As in *Duddy Kravitz*, the parallel items are often in grammatically asymmetrical forms: within an essentially serial form of language art, Richler tends to exploit pattern variety insistently, as his "D" value of 992 for *Hunting Tigers* attests (Appendix A: higher than all but two of the nonfiction samples). Numerals and numbers are once again numerous, with the *Hunting Tigers* sample topped on the nonfiction side only by that from *Shrug*.

Of all the elements of the style of *Duddy Kravitz* discussed here, only the densities of added clauses noted above and of freestanding nouns show major difference in the sample from *Hunting Tigers*. The first of these alterations, that of changing boundary, is perhaps the easiest of all the changes one can make in one's style. The second is perhaps an artifact of subject matter: instead of telling us about Irwin and Hersh and Duddy and Max, *Hunting Tigers* is often telling us about things that need a determiner or other modifier in order to stand up: the G, the Concord, the comic books, and even "Plimpton's uncommonly good" book.

The affinities are highly suggestive of what the true Richlerian syntax is and of how it is integrated with the generally collocative method of his art. It seems to me that to the ends of his art of collocation, Richler has fashioned a style distinctive in several aspects, most notably in its heavy reliance on nominal and paratactic devices. In the syntax of the man who uniquely relies on the noun, the noun phrase, the noun phrase series, we have truly an art of objects.

NOTES

1. See Graeme Gibson's interview of Richler in *Eleven Canadian Novelists*.

2. Notably Dennis Lee and W.J. Keith. At the Humanities Association of Canada meeting in 1973 (Kingston, Ontario) Lee said of *St. Urbain's Horseman* that Richler "lacks the moral clout" to deal with the serious issues raised by the book. For Keith see "Canadian Classics."

3. The other Richler novel centred on a cliché is *Cocksure*, in which the Star Maker reifies the cliché "Go fuck yourself."

4. Richler is a copious quoter of brand names, titles, foreignisms, numbers, and signs. The best case for his being a pop artist would come from *Hunting Tigers under Glass*, in which there are long stretches where nearly half the text consists of the five items listed above, plus similar impedimenta.

5. See Gibson's interview, and John Metcalf's.

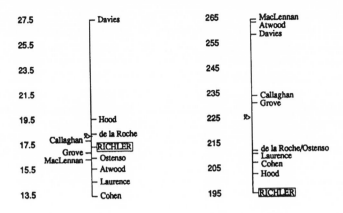

27.5	⊢ Davies		265	⊢ MacLennan
				⊢ Atwood
25.5			255	⊢ Davies
23.5			245	
21.5			235	⊢ Callaghan
				⊢ Grove
19.5	⊢ Hood		225	⊳
	⊢ de la Roche			
17.5	Callaghan ⊳ ⊢ RICHLER		215	⊢ de la Roche/Ostenso
	Grove ⊢ Ostenso			⊢ Laurence
	MacLennan ⊢			⊢ Cohen
15.5	⊢ Atwood		205	⊢ Hood
	⊢ Laurence			
13.5	⊢ Cohen		195	⊢ RICHLER

FIGURE 6.1

Average Period Length

FIGURE 6.2

Rankshifted Clauses per Sample

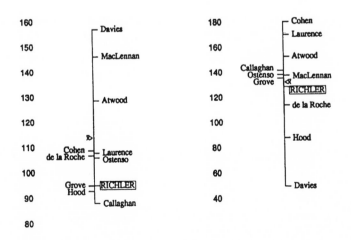

160	⊢ Davies		180	⊢ Cohen
				⊢ Laurence
150	⊢ MacLennan		160	⊢ Atwood
140			140	Callaghan ⊢ Ostenso ⊢ MacLennan
				Grove ⊲
130	⊢ Atwood		120	⊢ RICHLER
				⊢ de la Roche
120			100	
110	⊳ Cohen ⊢ Laurence		80	⊢ Hood
	de la Roche ⊢ Ostenso			
100			60	
	Grove ⊢ RICHLER			⊢ Davies
90	Hood ⊢ Callaghan		40	
80				

FIGURE 6.3

Finite Rankshifted Clauses per
Sample (42 + 43 + 00)

FIGURE 6.4

Periods with no Subordinator (42)
or Relative (43)

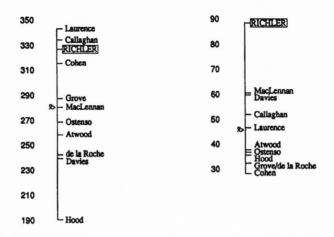

350 ─ Laurence	90 ─RICHLER
─ Callaghan	
330 ─RICHLER	80
─ Cohen	
310	70
	─ MacLennan
290 ─ Grove	60 ─ Davies
⅋─ MacLennan	
270 ─ Ostenso	50 ⅋─ Laurence ─ Callaghan
─ Atwood	
250	40 ─ Atwood ─ Ostenso ─ Hood
─ de la Roche	
─ Davies	
230	30 ─ Grove/de la Roche ─ Cohen
210	
190 ─ Hood	

FIGURE 6.5
Independent Clauses per Sample

FIGURE 6.6
And/or — *Added Independent
Clauses per Sample*

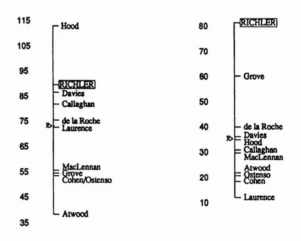

115 ─ Hood	80 ─RICHLER
105	70
95	60 ─ Grove
─RICHLER	
85 ─ Davies	50
─ Callaghan	
75 ─ de la Roche	40 ─ de la Roche
⅋─ Laurence	⅋─ Davies ─ Hood
65	30 ─ Callaghan ─ MacLennan
─ MacLennan	─ Atwood
55 ─ Grove	20 ─ Ostenso ─ Cohen
─ Cohen/Ostenso	
45	10 ─ Laurence
─ Atwood	
35	

FIGURE 6.7
Word Parallelism

FIGURE 6.8
Numbers and Numerals (81)

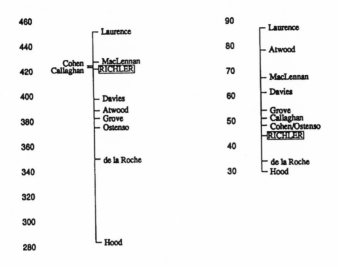

FIGURE 6.9
Finite Predicators

FIGURE 6.10
Tense Auxiliaries

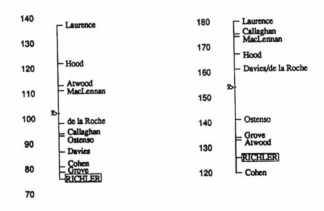

FIGURE 6.11
Function Adverbs (34)

FIGURE 6.12
Total Adverbs (04 + 34)

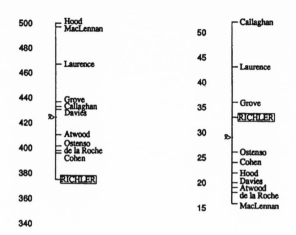

FIGURE 6.13
"M" Statistic
(03 + 04 + 33 + 34)

FIGURE 6.14
Postpositions (32)

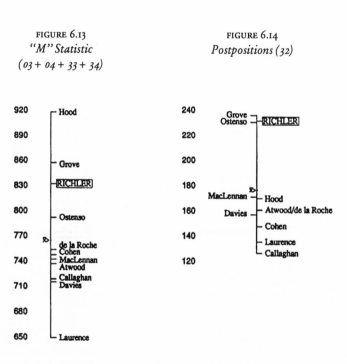

FIGURE 6.15
Nouns (01)

FIGURE 6.16
Freestanding Nouns

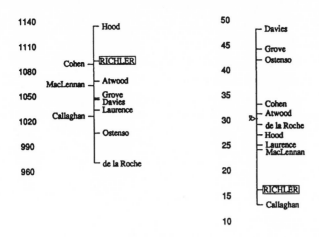

FIGURE 6.17
Nouns + Pronouns (01 + 11)

FIGURE 6.18
Relative Pronouns (43)

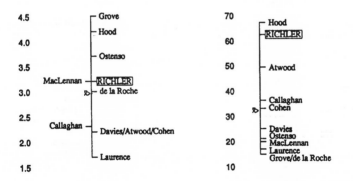

FIGURE 6.19
Noun : Pronoun Ratio (01 : 11)

FIGURE 6.20
Attributive Nouns (012)

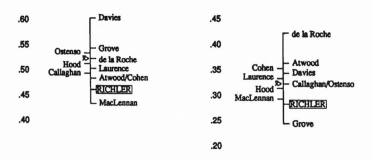

.60	┌ Davies
.55	┌ Grove
Ostenso ┤	├ de la Roche
Hood ⟋⟍	├ Laurence
.50 Callaghan	└ Atwood/Cohen
.45	─ RICHLER
	└ MacLennan
.40	

FIGURE 6.21
Determiner : Noun Ratio (31 : 01)

.45	
.40	┌ de la Roche
.35	├ Atwood
Cohen ┤	├ Davies
Laurence ⟋⟍	├ Callaghan/Ostenso
Hood	
.30 MacLennan	─ RICHLER
.25	└ Grove
.20	

FIGURE 6.22
Adjective : Noun Ratio (03: 01)

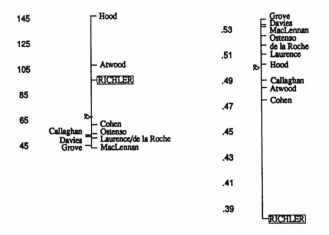

145	┌ Hood
125	
105	─ Atwood
	─ RICHLER
85	
65 ⟋⟍	┌ Cohen
Callaghan	├ Ostenso
Davies	├ Laurence/de la Roche
45 Grove	└ MacLennan

FIGURE 6.23
Noun Phrase Packers
(012 + 017 + 035)

	┌ Grove
.53	├ Davies
	├ MacLennan
	├ Ostenso
	├ de la Roche
.51	└ Laurence
⟋⟍	─ Hood
.49	┌ Callaghan
	└ Atwood
.47	─ Cohen
.45	
.43	
.41	
.39	
	└ RICHLER

FIGURE 6.24
Preposition : Noun Ratio (51 : 01)

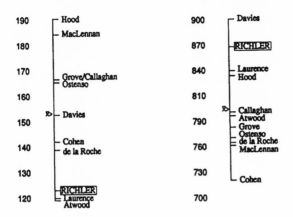

190	Hood	900	Davies
	MacLennan		
180		870	RICHLER
170	Grove/Callaghan	840	Laurence
	Ostenso		Hood
160		810	
150	⅀— Davies	790	⅀ Callaghan
			Atwood
			Grove
			Ostenso
140	Cohen	760	de la Roche
	de la Roche		MacLennan
130		730	
	RICHLER		Cohen
120	Laurence	700	
	Atwood		

FIGURE 6.25

Prepositional Phrases per Sample

(51-31-01)

FIGURE 6.26

"D" Statistic

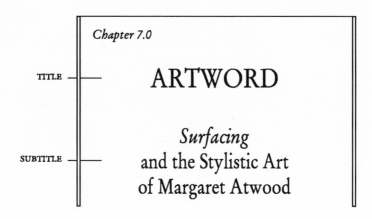

Chapter 7.0

TITLE

ARTWORD

SUBTITLE

Surfacing
and the Stylistic Art
of Margaret Atwood

A large body of criticism has grown up around the published works of Margaret Atwood. It is certain that no Canadian writer ever has had so much attention from graduate students and critics before turning 50. It is possible — nay, probable — that no Canadian writer living or dead has had so much of such attention, period. Why? Why Atwood?

One possible answer is quite simply that she deserves the attention. In my view, she shares with Eli Mandel the distinction of being Canada's biggest linguistic talent of the post-war years. She has a massive range of dialect and register, together with a level of syntactic control matched in my reading experience of post-1800 authors only by Woolcott Gibbs in his *New Yorker* pieces 50 years ago.[1] And she has taken bigger risks with language and art than either Mandel or Gibbs. She has earned her place in the critical limelight.

No more than a fraction of the attention lavished upon her has focused itself primarily on aspects of her language. Though she has repeatedly eschewed the role of political novelist and has made several public statements rejecting the notion that her books are "message" works with propositional content,[2] her use of nationalist and feminist themes as raw material has joined with her public personal support of various causes to make her work an object for those who would conscript art in the service of politics. Thematic treatments of her work — especially of themes relating to nationalism and feminism — abound.

Widespread among her critics is a tendency to get half way through an Atwood maze and imagine that a final goal of some kind has been reached. Early commentators on *Surfacing* were likely to seize on the book's anti-Americanism, interpreting "American" in a narrowly political rather than broadly figural sense.[3] Similarly Annis Pratt, in an archetypal-thematic treatment of *Surfacing*, remarks on the surfacer's "decision to get pregnant by Joe, whom she associates, archetypically, with a buffalo" (153). What Joe is in fact associated with is the buffalo on the obsolete U.S. nickel — Atwood's figure of thought here being a kind of Möebius-strip play on Nature and Art rather than the binary opposition that exists only in the critic's expectations. That Atwood has fed those expectations one does not deny, but the ironic management of her iconography does demand continuously careful handling of a sort it does not always get.

Besides the reflex responses and half-readings, there are nonreadings that are wholly surprising in the commentary on an author whose canon has been so saturated in critical ink. Two examples will suffice. The surfacer is an artist. Where is the commentary on the use of colour in the book? The *lacuna* seems egregious. And the title of *Life Before Man*, perhaps as rich as the title of *Love's Labour's Lost*: why, with the exception of Linda Hutcheon, has no critic chosen to give close scrutiny to the kaleidoscope quality of that three-word phrase? The *before* is more than temporal; it is also the *before* of "death before dishonor." *Life* here is more than prehistoric biosystems; it is also the vaginocentric Chthonic deities (and their language) overthrown by the party of Zeus when Athena came to the aid of *Man*,[4] to establish the Areopagus and together with it the primacy of the masculine language of reason and law. The manifold and layered suggestions in the title continue to work throughout the book, and I find it difficult to imagine an intelligent critical reading of the work that does not at least implicitly accept those suggestions as present from page one.

It seems inevitable that about a writer on whom more things have been written more bad things will have been written as well. There *is* good work. On the biographical and thematic sides, there have been the book by Jerome Rosenberg and the collection put together by the Davidsons, as well as the collection assembled by Sherrill Grace and

Lorraine Weir, and the single study by Grace alone. Scattered throughout these, *en passant*, are competent observations on Atwood's relationship with the language and with language, as well as on structural propensities in her work that we would include under the name of *style*.

I have yet to find any dissent to the proposition that Atwood's writing is strongly self-reflexive. This, among other elements in her art, makes her work "a garden of textual delights" to Frank Davey. Both Eli Mandel and Linda Hutcheon have taken note of that same self-reflexive impulse. Mandel uses it as an assumption in developing a line of reasoning that for the first two-thirds of his essay seems a mere bourgeois formalist excursion into Atwood's poems (there is text and only text and text wall to wall), but Mandel the self-reflexive critic does rather a U-turn and ends with politics. Hutcheon uses the self-reflexiveness as a point of departure to argue a thesis about the development of Atwood's style in fiction — a development "from poetic to narrative structures" — to which we shall return later in the chapter.

There is also wide agreement that Atwood chooses to deal with motifs and materials that produce exotic lexical features in her texts, giving rise to a number of unusual sets: the gothic, the grotesque, shamanism, tribal cults, as well as sets from other literary genres. Onto these offbeat constituents of the common vocabulary Atwood has grafted a "private" vocabulary the centre of which seems to me to be the ancient antithesis between Nature and Art. Hutcheon, Weir, and Davey have all studied the peculiar Atwood vocabulary and the various antitheses and sublanguages that lie embedded in it. Perforce it is a subject to which any stylistic analyst must sooner or later give due attention.

Scattered through her work — poems, novels, short stories, and even the criticism — are allegories of language and art that indicate a concern for language and language use that is both insistent and complex. Davey concludes his book with the statement (likely true) that "in Atwood's post-atomic and post-Adamic world . . . language has become metaphorically the world" (169).[5] Prominent among those allegories is the one in *Surfacing* that is the focus of this chapter, though there are many others as well. As Hutcheon notes, Atwood's novels tend to be about "identity and perception" (27). Language in the novels is the principal vehicle for developing and addressing the problems of identity and perception that are at the centre of the works.

At least from *The Circle Game* forward, Atwood has rejected not only ornateness and ornament (in the Ciceronian sense) but also the goals of persuasive clarity and reasoned explicitness that Cicero's forbears and inheritors (an all-male cast, incidentally) have so insistently pursued. *Survival* aside, her books seem opposed to that tradition, being as they are, "laconic, vivid, concrete in their imagery, disturbing in their juxtapositions" (Davey 27). George Woodcock ("Metamorphosis" 141) and Rosenberg have treated Atwood's reductive aesthetic of language almost as a question of economy of style. Others — notably Robert Lecker, Philip Stratford, and I — have treated it in *Surfacing* as something associated with deadness, with the loss of feeling undergone by the surfacer in her retreat from reason and civilization. In Davey's account — the most subtle and most resonant to date — her brevity and disjunctiveness are qualities developed as alternatives to the rational language we have inherited from the masculine tradition. Good language, in short, might be

oblique and enigmatic . . . a language structure of intrinsic attraction rather than one dependent on the action it narrates. It has the potential, in short, to act in the implicit way of 'female' language rather than in the explicit way of the male. (128)

A male critic, a reborn believer in the tradition of Aristotle and Cicero as transmitted through Quintilian, proceeding through texts with a rational system of syntactic categorization of Random Samples[6] of those texts, might readily think himself an unwelcome trespasser at these woods, suspected — perhaps even guilty — of attempting to invade, clear, and fence the mysterious wilderness and ultimately to pollute it. Before entering a plea or assembling evidence about the style of *Surfacing* in particular or about Atwood's style in general, I should restate that this analytic system cannot reason with any mysteries. All it can do is to make visible in the texts some important features of recursive structure that are only subtly visible to the naked eye. Perhaps, by making explicit some things that can be treated explicitly and by acknowledging that mystery is indeed something beyond, it makes a more proper act of obeisance to mystery than do other, less explicit and less systematic approaches. The question in any case is moot and will probably remain so.

The surfacer goes through her entire crisis — her journey to the wilderness, to the underworld and beyond — without a name. The fact of her namelessness is merely the first of several ways in which this text is linguistically minimized and stripped. There is also an insistent suppression of verbal variation. For example:

> Layer of leaves and needles, layer of roots, damp sand. That was what used to bother me most about the cities, the white zero-mouthed toilets in their clean tiled cubicles. Flush toilets and vacuum cleaners, they roared and made things vanish, at that time I was afraid there was a machine that could make people vanish like that too, go nowhere, like a camera that could steal not only your soul but your body also. Levers and buttons, triggers, the machines sent them up as roots sent up flowers; tiny circles and oblongs, logic become visible, you couldn't tell in advance what would happen if you pressed them. (117–18)

In a passage of barely 100 total items, there are 44 that are parts of one or another scheme of repetition: 16 different words in a total vocabulary of 77 different words. Six of the repeated items are lexemes: *layer, roots, toilets, vanish, machines,* and *sent up*. I strongly suspect that a concordance — quite apart from quantifying the recursion of dominant items such as *dead/death/die* and *drown/drowned/drowning* — would show *Surfacing* to have less variety in its words than nearly any other fiction of equivalent length written for an adult audience. The pronominal density of the work (one thing that we *have* quantified) is itself quite suggestive in this regard.[7] And, finally, there is the matter of *Surfacing*'s pecular and uniquely restricted syntax.

As anyone knows who has been to one of her readings, the peculiar lingering flavour of Atwood's poetry read aloud derives only partly from the text and its brutally skewed ikons. What truly stays with one is the remarkable bleached voice from which all devices of oral colouring have been ruthlessly laundered: the reading is given with no variation in either pitch or volume and with as little provision of stress as the English language will allow; the ikons hang starkly in the air, suspended almost as if self-willed, with no specifically human intervention.

She has done in *Surfacing* a very similar thing with the non-phonological resources of the language, especially the syntactic resources, the retrenchment of which gives the book a syntactic profile not only distinctive in the Atwood canon but unique in all 20th-century fiction. In no other writer than Atwood and in no other book than *Surfacing* has the range of these resources been so drastically inhibited. Clearly that inhibition is bound up with both the outer and the inner events that happen to the surfacer over the course of the novel; precisely how bound up will be easier to suggest after a description of the work's style and of its place in the development of Margaret Atwood as stylist. The comparison texts chosen for this chapter are listed in Table 7.1.

TABLE 7.1

Samples Used for Chapter 7

Atwood, *Surfacing*	Richler, *Duddy Kravitz*
Atwood, *Edible Woman*	Grove, *Fruits of the Earth*
Atwood, *Life Before Man*	Laurence, *The Stone Angel*
Davies, *Fifth Business*	Ostenso, *Wild Geese*
MacLennan, *Two Solitudes*	Callaghan, *Native Argosy/ Strange Fugitive*

The comparisons among these eleven texts were revealing, showing *Surfacing* to be truly distinctive in a wide variety of ways. The properties of the syntax of the York sample — its short clauses, its utter eschewing of the modifying words, its pronominality, its clause-end additions (participles and appositives), its nearly total avoidance of minus-additioned clauses — add up to a style distinguished not merely by the magnitude of its deviations but also by their sheer number. Yet, at the same time, it shows strong affinities with the two other samples from the Atwood canon.

CLAUSES AND CLAUSAL ARRAYS

This is a highly predicative text. *Surfacing* has a greater density of clauses of all types than any of the control texts except those of Callaghan. It also has a greater density of finite rankshifted clauses than any of the controls except MacLennan and Davies. These two facts (Figures 7.1 and 7.2) produce a paradox: a style of notable complexity wherein the average clause length (Figure 7.3) and even the average independent clause length (Figure 7.4) are short. Not only are the independent clauses short; where they contain dependencies, the dependent elements are nearly always right-branched rather than placed medially or frontally. Figure 7.5 shows for each of our texts the average point of first subordinator as a percentage of average length of independent clause.[8] *Surfacing* is clearly in the right-branched group, with Callaghan, Richler, Laurence, and the sample for *Edible Woman*. A few examples of Atwood's technique here may be illuminating:

> Finally she had to back down; he could fight, but only *if* they hit first.

> A mosquito lights on my arm and I let it bite me, *waiting* till its abdomen globes with blood before I pop it with my thumb like a grape.

> I look around at the walls, the window; it's the same, it hasn't changed, but the shapes are inaccurate *as though* everything has warped slightly.

> (*Sfg.* 72–73)

The monotone of short independent clauses is relieved somewhat by the right-branched rankshifted clauses that begin with the italicized words, but not much.

All three examples above, in addition to being right-branched, are compound-complex sentences. Moreover, of the five added independent clauses, only two are added in the normal way, syndetically (*and* in line 1 of the second sentence, *but* in line 2 of the third). This set of facts is typical of the *Surfacing* sample as a whole: not only does it offer more intrasentence full stops (colons and semicolons) than any other in the group (Figure 7.6), but its density of syndetically added independent clauses is less than two-thirds of the norm as number (Figure 7.7), barely half the norm as percent (Figure 7.8).[9] Though the sample has a large number of added clauses in it (Figure 7.9), it also has, next to the *Fifth Business* sample, the fewest periods without finite subordinate clauses in it — 76 — and ten of those 76 are fragments. The compound-complex sentence is often Atwood's sentence of choice.

Serial independent clauses, brief but complex, right-branched and arranged asyndetically, thus constitute the dominant feature of sentence design in this work. Those serial clauses are notably free of minus-additioning; in short, nearly every new clause gets a new subject, as Figure 7.10 suggests. Sentences like the following are not unusual in this text:

> I give David the machete, I don't know what shape the trail will be in, we may have to brush it out; Joe carries the hachet.
>
> It's overcast, lowhanging cloud; there's a slight wind from the southeast, it may rain later or it may miss us, the weather here comes in pockets, like oil.

(Sfg. 46)

Notice that each subject is likely to be followed immediately by its predicator phrase; this direct predication is more visible in this text and in *Life Before Man* than in any of our control writers except Grove (Figure 7.11). The avoidance of left-branched or medially placed adverbial elements that such a technique entails is simply one more aspect of an overall stylistic method designed to reduce colour, emphasis, and explicit connexion, at least at the syntactic level. Linguistic connexions, in short, are not to be trusted.

PREDICATION

Despite the clear and strong drive towards parataxis of short independent clauses and the great abundance of *finite* rankshifted clauses, Atwood does much of her right-branching with *non*finite clauses (Figure 7.13):

> I heard the mosquito whine of a motor *approaching*; I left my handful of crumbs on the tray and went out on the point *to watch*. It was Paul's boat, white-painted and squarish, hand-made; he waved to me from the stern. There was another man with him, *sitting* in the bow, backwards. (*Sfg.* 93)

The total of nonfinite forms in the *Surfacing* sample is exceeded among the non-Atwood samples only by those for Callaghan and

Grove (Figure 7.14). The title of the book itself is a nonfinite form, significantly open-ended and participial.

The text is strongly participial too, as Figures 7.15, 7.16, and 7.17 indicate. What the surfacer undergoes is a process, and process attracts *ing* verb-forms — not just participles (06) and participial adjectives (033) but ongoing-aspect verbs (023):

> What I'm seeing (023) is the black and white tugboat that used to be on the lake, or was it flat like a barge, it towed the log booms slowly down towards the dam, I waved at it whenever we went past in our boat and the men would wave back. It had a little house on it for them to live in, with windows and a stovepipe coming (06) out through the roof. I felt it would be the best way to live, in a floating (033) house carrying (06) everything you needed with you and some other people you liked . . . (*Sfg.* 40)

Those ongoing processes for the surfacer are largely passive or perceptual: she is *seeing, waiting, feeling, crying, watching, listening, checking*, and even *lying flat*. It is the others who are *approaching, invading, singing, making* the movie. Frequently the ongoing is simply a negative, a non-event, or a hypothetical:

> I shouldn't be *going* by myself . . . (74)

> . . . if he'd been *wearing* a hat he would have taken it off. (94)

> Into my head the tugboat floated, the one that was on the lake before, logboom *trailing* it, men *waving* from the cabin . . . (119)

The surfacer often appears to us as recumbent or static:

> I lie for a while with my eyes open. (42)

Accordingly, the density of finite be-forms and passives is very nearly equal to that in *Fifth Business* (Figure 7.18). The passage immediately above continues:

> . . . This *used to be* my room; Anna and David *are* in the one with the map, this one has the pictures. Ladies in exotic costumes, sausage rolls of hair across their foreheads, with puffed red mouths and eyelashes like toothbrush bristles: when I *was* ten I believed in glamour, it was a kind of religion and these *were* my icons. Their arms and legs *are constrained* in fashion-model poses . . . .

A major distinction of *Surfacing* as a text is its predicative density.

And within that density both process and state — i.e. passive state — are strongly foregrounded. We should expect as much from the development of the plot.

PHRASES

Surfacing, in keeping with the general colourlessness of its prose, is of all the texts the sparest in modification. But we still are confronted with a high density of a restricted few of the modifying devices that go with nouns. Figures 7.19 through 7.21 illustrate some noun-modifying word-class groups, together with the overall adverb count in 7.22.

Like her independent clauses, Atwood's noun phrases in *Surfacing* tend to be right-branched. The work shows, to an extent more than double the mean for the controls, a strong propensity for apposition and postmodification (Figure 7.20). For example:

The sound of love in the north, a *kiss*, a *slap*.

We pass gigantic stumps, *level* and *saw-cut* . . .

I watch for the blazes, still *visible* after 14 years . . . (58)

Within the monotone strings of clauses, seemingly stripped bare of all except their subject-predicator openings, the phrase structures have been plucked truly clean. The adjective phrases rarely have either adverbs or intensifiers (Figure 7.22); the noun phrases lack attributive adjectival modification. *Surfacing*, in fact, has the third lowest modifier total of the more than 280 texts that our team has analyzed from the last 337 years, i.e. since Thomas Hobbes's *Leviathan*. Such restraint of modification — atypical in Atwood's work — is simply one more aspect of the wholly conscious system of reduction of colouration so prominent in *Surfacing*'s style.

A further aspect of that system can be seen in a consideration of syntactic variety. The York Inventory's "D" statistic measures, indirectly, variety at the level of phrase structure. A normal "D" for a present-day writer is in the mid-800s, though in the long perspective of history there is a lot of variation around the present-day mean: Sidney and Milton come in around 1,200; the King James Version of the *Psalms* is the all-time low-water mark at 450, a depth almost reached by Edward Gibbon in *The Decline and Fall of the Roman Empire*. Atwood's "D" of 718 in *Surfacing*, is the second lowest in the York Inventory since Gibbon's autobiography (Figure 7.24).

SYNTAX AND THE ART OF THE BOOK

Like Atwood's other "female comedies" (Davey 57-80) *Surfacing* presents a crisis in the development of a female protagonist. Unlike the others, it involves a purifying passage through something very like a schizophrenic episode (n.b. "Some of your lines are double" *Sfg*. 8). That episode is marked geographically by retreat into a wilderness which, though exploited, is largely untamed;[10] it is marked socially by the abandonment of companions, cooked food, and all other concomitants of "society" and "civilization," even clothing and tools. The minimally varied lexis and the restricted syntax that mark the book's style are major elements in the rejection of all that is civilized, masculine, American, or industrial. In short, language in its conventional sense and conventional uses becomes one of the book's negatives.

In order to become whole, the surfacer must read the "new meaning" of the rock paintings (158), but first she has to "immerse [herself] in the other language." As for the child conceived at the beginning of part 3, she will "never teach it any words" (162). Ultimately she proclaims the possibility of her redemption and renewal: "I no longer have a name. I tried for all those years to be civilized but I'm not and I'm through pretending" (168). The minimalist character of the style of the book and its frequent fragmentation (Figure 7.23) offer us an alternative language to the ornate, masculine, coherent language of the rhetorical tradition.

There is finally the business of both clausal and phrasal right-branching — the apposition, the postmodification, the tendency to use subordinate clauses in situations where they will terminate rather than begin a sentence. Just as the novel itself embodies a process of discovery, so do the surface structures of its syntax. Things are not named; they are discovered, discovered even in parataxis:

The forest thickens and I watch for the blazes, still visible after fourteen years; the trees they've cut on have grown swollen edges around the wounds, scar tissue. (46)

It is difficult, in connexion with the book's extraordinary appositional quality, not to think of *Heart of Darkness*, another journey into self-discovery in which a similar syntactic strategy is similarly foregrounded.

THE STYLE OF SURFACING AND THE STYLE OF ATWOOD

This book is not just different in style from other Atwood novels, it is in some ways radically so. Of all the writers of English since 1800, I know of but one other who in mid-career was able to effect conscious changes in his style of the magnitude wrought by Atwood in *Surfacing* — Thomas Carlyle.

The other two Atwood fiction texts used in this chapter are generally more "normal" than *Surfacing* in the quanta they produce. Several figures in this chapter illustrate the fact: Total Clauses (7.1), Finite Rankshifted Clauses (7.2), Average Clause Length (7.3), Noun & Pronoun Subjects (7.10), Participles (7.15), Attributive Nouns (7.19), Total Adverbs (7.22), and, finally, "D" Statistic (7.24). In all these measures, *Edible Woman* and *Life Before Man* fall much closer to the mean. Do all the radical changes somehow make *Surfacing* a special, anomalous case within the Atwood canon? Paradoxically, the answer to that question is negative, for *Surfacing* can be seen to be a natural point in the development of Atwood's style, a mid-point between *Edible Woman* and *Life Before Man*.

There are several ways in which Atwood's style starts out different from the control group in the first book (*EW*), becomes more so in the second (*Sfg.*), and even more so in the third (*LBM*). That style is first of all clausally complex, achieving much of its complexity through nonfinite forms (Figures 7.25, 7.26). Second, it deals with process, process being manifested through participials and other *ing*-forms, and it tends to become more process-oriented with each book (Figures 7.27, 7.28). Though the early works deal much with states (Figure 7.30), especially with passive states (Figure 7.29), this tendency diminishes with time. Concurrently, the noun phrases get larger (Figure 7.31), so that what produces a copulative clause in an earlier work (e.g. *Surfacing*'s "his hands at any rate *are* intelligent . . ." [68]) may produce simply an attributive noun or a postmodifier later: "arms hugging the bolster shapes of each other's winter coats" (*LBM* 111). The tendency towards apposition and postmodification is present from the beginning and grows stronger with time, as does her preference for adding clauses asyndetically and her rejection of explicit clause-to-clause connexion.

There are also ways in which *Edible Woman* is "normal" and the two later works more distinctive and deviant. There is nothing unusual in Atwood's amount of direct predication until the second novel, and the extensive use of fragmentation that first appears in *Surfacing* seems, by *Life Before Man*, to have become an important aspect of her language-handling technique, perhaps even an aesthetic principle.[11]

In sum, even though it is of a piece with our other two works from the Atwood canon, *Surfacing* can be seen to be both distinctive and deliberately eccentric within that canon. In its style it is the most radical exploration of the view formulated by Davey:

> The troubles of the world . . . are all in a sense linguistic problems that stem from Adamic language and its arbitrary and distorting imposition on experience. (169)

But it is only the most radical manifestation of a style that has a number of clear directions built into it to begin with and being developed within it as it matures. As that style sheds metaphor in favour of other kinds of iconography, and as it moves away from the passive and static towards the ongoing and towards more directly apprehended action, it seems indeed to be moving, as Hutcheon has said, from poetic towards narrative structures.

SENSE, LEXIS, AND GENRE

Just as language is often suppressed within Atwood's style, so is hearing within the novels, except as an organic adjunct to the ubiquitous telephone. Another sense, taste, where it exists at all exists in attenuated or offended form — "identical gray hamburgers and mud gravy" or the city's "acid taste of copper wiring." Atwood characters don't enjoy their sex a whole lot; they are likely to enjoy their food even less. Smell exists for cellar mould and industrial fumes. The master sense of Atwood is sight, the master instruments of sense the eyes. And even where unseeing — as on Marian's cake or in the surfacer's childhood drawings — they are important. The optic nerve, passive, organic, and living, might even be the feminine cognate of the invasive, image-fixing, masculine camera.[12] Sight, unlike language, is natural.

The two principal lexical groups in Atwood are the embodiment of antithetic principles, and the antitheses — largely overlapping and mutually inclusive — are masculine-feminine and Art-Nature. The antithesis of dead-living, which of course has strong resonances within the other two, is also prominent, especially in *Life Before Man*. We often get the poles of these antitheses in mixed form — *viz.* Joe and the buffalo on the U.S. nickel, or David, whose eyes gleam like the bottoms of test-tubes. Art, or the industrial, is often grafted on to Nature, or the organic, often by violence, and the mixed effects can be ironic. In the nameless town that is "the last or first outpost" for the nameless protagonist of *Surfacing*, she remembers the canned peas in one of the two nameless restaurants as "watery and pallid as fisheyes," and the french fries as "bleary with lard" (*Sfg.* 7: there go those eyes again). She also has a curious kind of recollection that is an emblem not only of the recapitualitive processes she undergoes through much of the book but of the recognition and reversal that are the book's crisis and resolution:

> In one of those restaurants before I was born my brother got under the table and slid his hands up and down the waitress's legs while she was bringing the food; it was during the war and she had on shiny orange rayon stockings, he'd never seen them before, my mother didn't wear them. (7)

The waitress is industrially packaged, encased in things unnatural, but the mother that the protagonist is to rediscover feeding the birds at the end of the book "didn't wear them." And it is not even a first-hand memory. Or is it?

The Art-Nature antithesis can be traced to classical pastoral,[13] of which the most distinguished descendent in the prose of the Modern English Period is Sir Philip Sidney's *Arcadia*. Other, more recent, descendents include a long passage in West's *Miss Lonelyhearts* and

James Dickey's economic and artistic tour-de-force *Deliverance*.[14] Classical pastoral is anti-romantic, anti-Rousseau, anti-Wordsworth in character. In it, Nature is threatening; Art is redemptive, keeping the jungle at bay. Sidney's Duke Basileus and his retinue of followers fall into disorder and misrule when they move to the country, as does his urban dukedom after his departure. Dickey's bourgeois Atlanta suburbanites undergo terror, sodomy-rape, permanent injury, and even death in their retreat into the wilds. In both works, the would-be woodsmen return to civilization and are better off for the return. They learn they don't belong "out there." Happiness is order, law 'n' order: two Chevrolets and a quarter acre of manicured lawn. In *Surfacing*, Atwood makes a tidy and ambiguous play on the conventions of pastoral as *genre*. For three of her four principals, the pastoral is wholly classical. David, Anna, and Joe are misfits in Nature: Anna's obsessively made-up face, made up for David, belongs in the province of Art. Only the surfacer herself can hope to belong, and only after learning "the other language," the Nature-language of fusion (female), to replace the Art-language of distinction (male). And even she, ultimately, must return to the city, though a sadder and wiser woman. She alone of the book's characters can emerge from the pastoral experience with anything of value. She alone can know that the animals have no need for speech.

CONCLUSIONS

Atwood has the linguistic resources and the poetic training and self-discipline to write any way she wants. Her right-branching asyndetic books are likely to be voyages of discovery, with the syntax at sentence level reflecting the larger movements of the work as a whole. The syntactic choices are as carefully made as in any other living writer. In many writers, even many writers that are outstanding artists, style is largely dependent on reflex developed before age 25. Not so Atwood, who has managed to develop a style — especially in *Surfacing* — that even down to its syntactic structures is a declaration of independence from the reasoning bonds of masculine form.

1. Gibbs's parodies probably show the keenest sense of syntax and the broadest grasp of trope of any parodies written in English. His fellow staffer E.B. White, whose name has been linked to the subject of style more often and more lucratively than anyone else's in the last 30 years, could not lift Gibbs's typewriter. For a measure of how good each one was, consider their efforts directed at a common target, Ernest Hemingway: Gibbs's "Death in the Rumble Seat" and White's "Across the Street and into the Grill."

2. *Vide* Atwood's letters ("A Reply") in *Signs: A Journal of Women in Culture and Society*, and in *Saturday Night* ("Lives").

3. See Atwood's interview with Graeme Gibson in *Eleven Canadian Novelists* 5-31.

4. The ultimate celebration of this overthrow is Aeschylus's trilogy, *Oresteia*.

5. A somewhat similar set of concerns is addressed in Donna Gerstenberger, "Conceptions Literary and Otherwise: Women Writers and the Modern Imagination."

6. "Random Samples" is the title of David's "film"-in-progress in *Surfacing*.

7. *Surfacing*'s pronoun total (433) and per cent (13.1) are both second highest of any of the 300+ samples in the inventory, Twain's *Tales* (at 451 and 13.6%) being tops. The mean for the Canadian fiction samples used in this book is around 300, or 8.9%. The nonpossessive forms of six words overwhelmingly dominate the group, to the extent of 95%: *I, you, he, she, it, they.*

8. Figures in excess of 100% are not anomalies. Consider a model:

John is tall. John is charming. John is popular but he doesn't play poker with the boys because he considers them boorish.

The average IC in this passage is 5.5 words. The point of first subordination for the one subordinator is word 13. The fraction produced by dividing first subordinator point by average IC would be 13 over 5.5, or 236%.

9. Much has been made in the past of Atwood's use of the "run-on sentence," especially in *Surfacing* — a sentence in which two successive independent clauses are joined only by a comma, without a coordinator. We do not treat such commas as intrasentence full stops.

10. There is no "pure" wilderness in *Surfacing*. Note: "Now we're passing the turnoff to the pit the Americans hollowed out. From here it looks like an innocent hill, spruce covered, but the thick power lines running into the forest give it away" (*Sfg.* 9).

11. We tested the possibility that there would be different degrees of fragmentation from narrator to narrator among the three main characters of *Life Before Man*. Within our sample we could find nothing conclusive — each character having a minimum of five fragments in his/her third of the sample (1100 words). A count for the book as a whole, with a count for each of the three narrators, might well reveal differences.

12. See Davey on "An Atwood Vocabulary," and Barbara Blakely, "The Pronunciation of Flesh: A Feminist Reading of Atwood's Poetry."

13. For a capsule history, see William Edward Tayler, *Nature and Art in Renaissance Literature*.

14. Dickey planned *Deliverance* from the beginning as a source of economic independence and of liberation from the college/university lecture/reading circuit, where he often seasoned his performances with a salty but cheerful detestation of both students and professors. At York in 1969, fortified by a litre or so of Kentucky courage, he outlined to a group of four or five of us his plan for the book, which included "400 grand at least" for the film rights "plus a piece of the gross" and "a part in the damn thing — I mean an acting part." Heard in the context of these remarks, the title of the work picks up some base notes not immediately audible to the unaided ear. His auditors discovered later that his plan was not merely the work of a hyperactive Fancy lubricated by Bourbon. Dickey delivered. And so, apparently, did his agent.

FIGURE 7.1
Total Clauses per Sample

FIGURE 7.2
*Finite Rankshifted Clauses
per Sample*

FIGURE 7.3
Average Clause Length

FIGURE 7.4
*Average Independent
Clause Length*

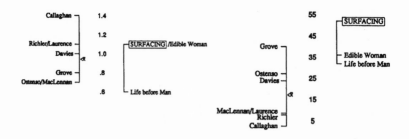

FIGURE 7.5
First Subordinator Point as %
of Average IC *Length*

FIGURE 7.6
Intrasentence Full Stops (98)

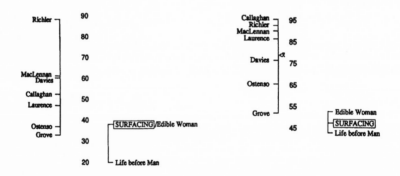

FIGURE 7.7
Syndetically Added ICs
(Initial 41 & Added ICs)

FIGURE 7.8
Syndetically Added Clauses as
% of all Added Clauses

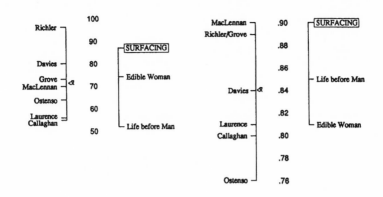

FIGURE 7.9
And/or — *Added Independent Clauses + Internal Full Stops (98)*

FIGURE 7.10
Noun and Pronoun Subjects as % of Finite Predicators

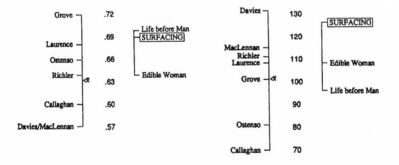

FIGURE 7.11
Direct Predication as % of all Finite Predicators

FIGURE 7.12
Word Parallelism

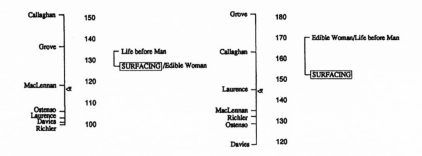

FIGURE 7.13
Nonfinite Clauses
(05 + 06 + 07)

FIGURE 7.14
Total Nonfinite Forms

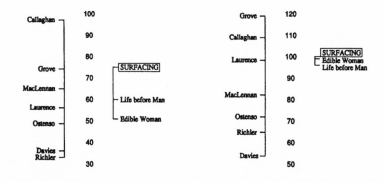

FIGURE 7.15
Participles (06)

FIGURE 7.16
Participles & Participial Adjectives
(06 & 033)

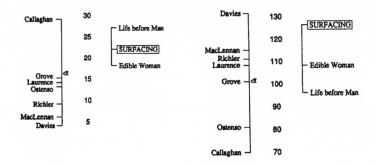

FIGURE 7.17
Ongoing Aspect Verbs (023)

FIGURE 7.18
Finite be forms + Finite
Passives (213 + 022)

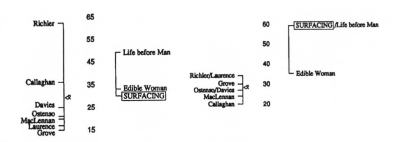

FIGURE 7.19
Attributive Nouns (012)

FIGURE 7.20
Appositives + Postmodifiers
(017 + 035)

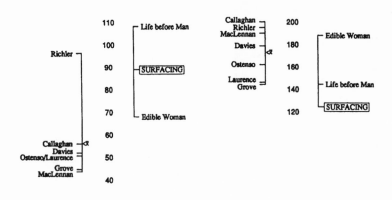

FIGURE 7.21
Total Noun Phrase Packers
(012 + 017 + 035)

FIGURE 7.22
Total Adverbs + Intensifiers
(04 + 34 + 33)

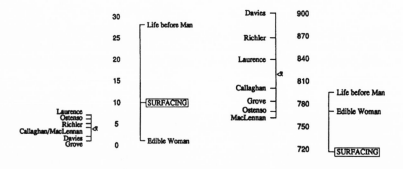

FIGURE 7.23
Sentence Fragments (995)

FIGURE 7.24
"D" Statistic

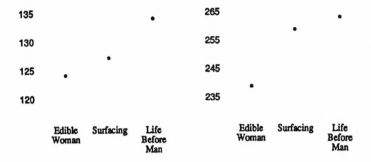

135   •

130

125   •

120

       Edible   Surfacing   Life
       Woman   Before
                         Man

265   •

255   •

245

235   •

       Edible   Surfacing   Life
       Woman   Before
                         Man

FIGURE 7.25 (ATWOOD'S DEVELOPMENT)
Nonfinite Clauses per Sample
(05 + 06 + 07)

FIGURE 7.26 (ATWOOD'S DEVELOPMENT)
Rankshifted Clauses per Sample

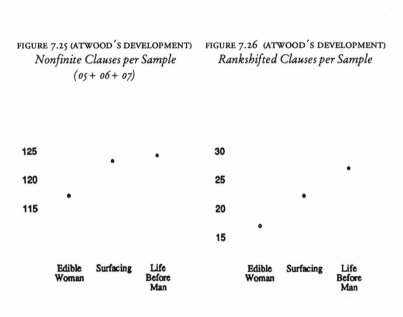

FIGURE 7.27 (ATWOOD'S DEVELOPMENT)
Participial Forms (06 + 023 + 033)

FIGURE 7.28 (ATWOOD'S DEVELOPMENT)
Ongoing Aspect Verbs (023)

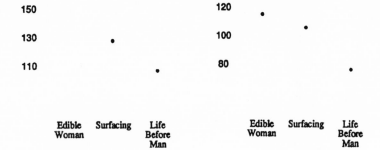

150	●				120		●		
130			●		100			●	
110				●	80				●

| Edible Woman | Surfacing | Life Before Man | | | Edible Woman | Surfacing | Life Before Man |

FIGURE 7.29 (ATWOOD'S DEVELOPMENT)
Finite be *(213) + Passives (022)*

FIGURE 7.30 (ATWOOD'S DEVELOPMENT)
Finite be *forms (213)*

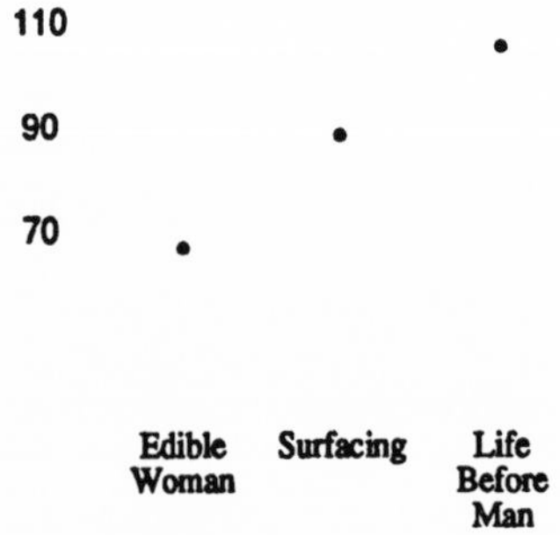

110		●
90	●	
70	●	

| Edible Woman | Surfacing | Life Before Man |

FIGURE 7.31 (ATWOOD'S DEVELOPMENT)
Noun Phrase Packers

SECTION — Conclusions

Part 3.0

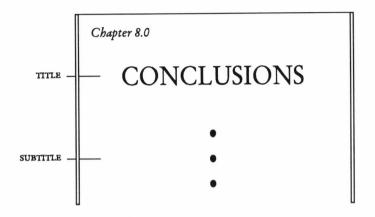

Chapter 8.0

TITLE

CONCLUSIONS

•
•
•

SUBTITLE

CANADA AND THE CANADIAN STYLE

In a gathering of language teachers in Toronto in 1975, Louis T. Milic, the eminent linguist from just south of Lake Erie, managed to stun us all with the following statement: "Canadian English? There is no such thing. What you have here is only a variety of American English, with few points of distinction if any. I could walk from Niagara Falls to the shore of Hudson Bay without crossing a single isogloss." In true Canadian style, we all felt it would be ill-mannered to disagree with our guest, and we let the remark pass without discussion. One must hope that we would not respond that way today and that outside of Canada, at least among serious academics, such notions are less likely to pass muster now than they were in the mid-1970s. The study of Canadian English is both serious and established.

That study has concentrated first on phonology and to a lesser extent on matters of vocabulary.[1] It is undeniable that Canadian English differs from other national branches of the mother stock, and that within Canada there is significant, specifically Canadian, regional variation. But the matter of a Canadian Style is still an open question, even if we accept as a working premise the partial fallacy of temporal and/or national stylistic types (Bridgman).

Despite the existence of highly ornate, non-conversational, embedding writers such as Milton, Clarendon, and Robert Boyle during the Restoration it is possible to admit the general and somewhat flabby term, "Restoration Style" to refer to right-branching, hypotactic, conversational styles such as those of Dryden, Robert Howard, Abraham Cowley, and Thomas Sprat. Likewise, despite the existence of syntactic gargoyle-builders like Henry James and Frederick Buechner and of baroque exterior decorators like Nabokov and Updike, one can speak of "The American Style" and be understood to be referring to a set of direct, informally conversational, "simple" tricks of using language that arise in Twain and come through to the present generation of practitioners by way of Stein, Hemingway, and Anderson. But it seems to me that there is not yet enough *stuff* for us to speak, even fallaciously, of *a* Canadian Style or *the* Canadian Style. There is not yet a sufficient mass of reputable prose writers all doing some of the same things or several highly similar things, such as Dryden and his crowd in the late 1600s or Stein and her crowd in the 1920s and 1930s. This is not to say that nothing can be said in general about Canadian style; there are some general observations that can be made, but they are not typological ones.

I would make three observations about the Canadian styles that we have examined in the York Inventory, i.e. the styles represented by the 53 samples detailed in Appendix A. First, they are generally more utilitarian, less decorated, less literary than the styles contemporary to them in the U.K. and the U.S. There are exceptions: Atwood is an obvious one. She is a very learned woman, and the framework of literary allusion in both her poetry and her prose is considerable. She and other writer-critics now working (Kroetsch, Bowering, Godfrey) may ultimately bend Canadian literary language in two ways: first, towards indirection, economy, minimalism; second, towards self-conscious, self-reflexive "literariness." Time will tell.

Second, several Canadian stylists (three of the four considered closely in this book) show, to an extent that is impressive, strong elements of influence from outside of Canada. The melting pot ethic has not been important in Canadian life, and this fact might well be reflected in the styles of our writers. If Davies, Richler, and Callaghan have been marching, in high Arnoldian fashion, to the beat of some collective drummer, it is not the Canadian National one. In a country that is culturally and politically centrifugal, writers may understandably wish to get closer to some place else than they have been inclined to do in the U.S.A. — James, Pound, Eliot notwithstanding.

Third — and this is reiteration of something said in detail in chapter 2 — the general drift of the literary language of Canada, the direction in which history seems to be taking us, shows strong kinship with the general drift of the language elsewhere in the English-speaking world, and that drift is away from France towards Germany, away from ornament towards utility and matter.

For those whose minds are unduly troubled by the messiness of reality, who require a *Zeitgeist* or a distillation of the ineffabilities of the national *Heldenstuff* at the end of any *Kulturgeschichtung*, I can right now offer nothing further, and I am sorry. More ambitious generalizations than those above await further study and further excursions into the data by other scholars.

THE DISCOURSE OF STYLE

A few years ago, in STYLE, Robert Adolph published an *Apologia pro Vita Sua* that incidentally included two assertions touching on matters central to the study of style: 1) that discussing style by typology, especially by referential typology (Senecan, Ciceronian, etc.), is both valid and useful; 2) that there can be a history of style, and a very good way — perhaps the best way — to go about that is *via* comparative translations. These notions deserve some passing attention, for in dealing with them he did, I believe, rather exaggerate the differences current between us on these points, and I would not wish for his version of my position to be among the last items in the printed record. I hope I have not misrepresented *him*.

First, stylistic types. Types are approximations. As I have indicated two pages back, with "Restoration" and "American," there are simply too many exceptions for most typological terms to have any viability in serious discussion. Moreover, with notions such as Senecan and Ciceronian or Tacitean we are dealing with stylistic paradigms from another language, a dead language — in short, with metaphorical notions. Now, only the most positivistic among us would exclude metaphor from the resources available to stylistic criticism; it conveys essences in a way that eludes technical terminology, and its use is sanctioned by the practice of eminent commentators for roughly two millenia. Senecan and Ciceronian, too, have been in use for centuries, at least for most of the duration of the Modern English Period. Not even the most thorough campaign for purity in thought and word is going to expunge them from the discourse of stylistic criticism, just as no campaign seems likely to expunge Classic and Romantic from our discussions of poetry. But we should be mindful of where such terminological dodo-birds belong — in the exordium, not in the body of the text — for they are preliminary and primitive rather than final descriptions of what the visible properties are of a particular style or a particular poetic text.

Second, the matter of a history of style by translation. Translation — both the theory and the practice thereof — is an important area of literary history, especially of the literary history of the 16th and 17th centuries. Its impact on the development of literary English in the early modern period is pervasive, and no intelligent history of poetry or prose in English can ignore it. But it is only a small part of any history of stylists (or, if you insist, of style). To attempt a history of stylists or style that focuses only on translators and translations would be like attempting a sociology of Canada that focuses exclusively on those who drive the Cadillac, the Mercedes, or the bmw. The objection is not that these people are not a telling and important part of the picture, important far beyond their numbers: it is that they are less, a great deal less, than the whole picture.

The first stylistics was that of the Greeks and Romans, revived by the humanists of the Renaissance. A second revival, contemporary stylistics, is now about 75 years old, having had its beginning in Morris Croll's neoclassical study of the prose styles of the English Renaissance and the 17th century. For the fifty years after Croll's first studies the names are few but distinguished: Wimsatt, R.F. Jones, Williamson, Harry Levin, Harold C. Martin, E.J.P. Corbett. The common ground among them is that they are all essentially literary scholars. In the mid-1950s, two other groups began to focus their energies on questions of style: statisticians (Mosteller, Wallace, Andrew Q. Morton) and serious students of language, most fruitfully the neo-Firthian systemicists in England (Halliday, Spencer, Gregory). So that modern stylistics exists somewhere near the middle among the camps of three not always congenial special interests: the study of literature, the formal study of probability, and the formal study of language. Attempts to capture the study of style and drag it off to be the exclusive property of one camp or another should be resisted. Though the middleness of stylistics has made it an easy target, that middleness is an essential part of its character as an interdiscipline and should be retained, perhaps even cherished, at least until literature departments renounce their abandonment of the serious and systematic study of language.

Whatever is said of style ought generally to meet the criteria of accuracy and relevance that prevail in the best humanistic scholarship. It ought, where quantitative in its evidence, to be prepared to meet tests of validity, reliability, and verifiability that are current among students of probability. It must also, without abandoning its distinguished classical past, adopt a vocabulary that is hospitable to those descriptive and interpretive insights of modern linguistics most salient in the study of literature.

This last is not an easy matter. The terms of the classical rhetoric — metaphor, antithesis, allegory, metonymy, and the like — are durable and can be presumed to be safe, even from Professor Chomsky. The big problem is novelty: there are too many descriptions of the language. The best of them for the study of style is Halliday's, which not only recognizes lexis and syntax and the interrelations between them but also has attempted to address many of the non-linguistic aspects of language and human interaction that arise from the origins of language as a social artifact. A universal adoption of Professor Halliday's framework might be too much to hope for, but the undertaking of such an adoption would give us the best chance since the time of Quintilian for extending and sharpening the communal vocabulary of style that we have inherited from the Greeks.

FURTHER STUDIES IN THIS MODE

The York Computer Inventory of Prose Style began on the basis of a surface-structure string grammar, and the original focal interest of the project was in parses of texts and incidences of particular word-classes. In the 20 years since we began, we have updated, modified, and expanded several times, and with each modification we have attempted to bend the project in a Hallidayan direction.[2] The present challenge for this system of analysis lies in the building of some semantic categories into the coding. I believe we will meet that challenge successfully. The old objection to the inclusion of a semantic layer — cost — may no longer be applicable, since it now appears that much of the text parse can be automated, perhaps to the extent of 75% of the labour involved in that most labour-intensive aspect of the research.[3]

In the last 20 years there have been massive developments in computer technology. There are microprocessors easily and cheaply available with more core than the IBM 360 mainframe computer on which we began this research in 1968. More elegant programming languages and more elegant ways of handling them are also readily available. Dr. Carpenter's program remains a remarkable piece of work: over 2200 statements in Fortran IV for the G compiler. With present-day technology he will be able to do a lot more in less space.

Already Ian Lancashire and Lidio Presutti[4] have been able to modify our original programs to take natural language and parse concurrently, so that the computer instead of reading this —

311 031 031 015 021 514 311 031 019 991

will read this —

The/311/quick/031/brown/031/fox/015/jumped/021
/over/514/the/311/lazy/ 031/dog/019/PPP/991/

Potential gains in flexibility and in density of information are staggering. One will be able to get not only an instant *index verborum* of any text sample (with or without function words), but a count of particular words or particular groups in specified grammatical and/or semantic functions. One will be able also to perform instant collocational analysis of any specified word.

The next round of research in this mode will be done on a PC or on a desktop terminal that is part of a small network; storage will be on soft disk. The entire apparatus — programs, texts, parses — will take up less than a tenth of the space required by the tape storage we have used for the last 17 years and less than a hundredth of that required by the 80-column cards with which our project began. Portability and ease of use will be increased manyfold, though it will continue to be necessary for researchers to remain in close touch with one another because new coding decisions on idioms have to be made continually (and sometimes arbitrarily) and because each new writer is in some ways a whole new grammar.

It is now 25 years since Milic began feeding Fries-based parse into the Columbia University computer for his dissertation (later his book) on Swift. Many syntactic studies and many concordances have followed — some of them excellent, others a waste of time.[5] But out of all this work have emerged some clear ideas about what kinds of information can be derived from text with electronic assistance. The value of such information somehow continues to be mooted, obvious though it be to me that such information, obtainable in no other way, can lead us to much that is interpretively illuminating. The new technologies associated with the desktop computer hold marvelous possiblities. And though many *belletristes* regard them as constituting a potentially terminal day for literary studies, those of us who have worked in this area can see a massive expansion of opportunity close at hand.

NOTES

1. Notably the work during the 1950s, '60s, and early '70s by Walter Avis of the Royal Military College and by Jack Chambers of the University of Toronto.

2. The movement lies in the Inventory's increasing interest in clause types and clause structure. Fries's original grammar was defined 95% in terms of word-slots rather than in terms of larger structures and the functions within them.

3. Professor Graham Hirst, of the University of Toronto, together with his graduate students, is doing very interesting work on problems of autoparsing and machine translation.

4. Ian Lancashire and Lidio Presutti, of the Centre for Computing in the Humanities, University of Toronto, have already produced a version of the York Program for use on a DEC-10 computer that eliminates 40% of the labour in parsing by establishing a dictionary for each sample so that every *and* is coded 41x, every *the* 311, every *a* 313, etc.

5. Of conspicuous and exemplary excellence in a field that has seen mediocre work done on figures as major as Eugene O'Neill is the book/program by Herbert J. Donow, *A Concordance to the Sonnet Sequences of Daniel, Drayton, Shakespeare, Sidney, and Spenser.* In it, only the lexemes are given in context; function words are counted but not contextualized (a great space saver, this). The program is in three detachable parts: concordance for lexemes, *index verborum* for lexemes, *index verborum* for function words. With only minor modification, one could produce a concordance of the function words as well, if that were one's wish. Would that all concordance-makers had given the problems the same amount and quality of forethought!

WORKS CITED

Adolph, Robert. "On the Possibility of a History of Prose Style." STYLE 15:4 (1981): 435–50.

_____ . *The Rise of Modern Prose Style*. Cambridge, MA: MIT, 1968.

Atwood, Margaret. *The Edible Woman*. New York: Popular Library, 1969.

_____ . *Life Before Man*. Toronto: McClelland, 1979.

_____ . "Lives of the Poets" *Saturday Night* 92.1 (1977): 38–43

_____ . "A Reply." *Signs: A Journal of Women in Culture and Society* 2.2 (1976): 340–41.

_____ . *Surfacing*. Toronto: McClelland, 1972.

_____ . *Survival: A Thematic Guide to Canadian Literature*. Toronto: Anansi, 1972.

Berton, Pierre. *The Last Spike: The Great Railway, 1881–1885*. Toronto: McClelland, 1971.

_____ . *The Smug Minority*. Toronto: McClelland, 1968.

Blakely, Barbara. "The Pronunciation of Flesh: A Feminist Reading of Atwood's Poetry." Grace 33–52.

Bloom, Allan. *The Closing of the American Mind*. New York: Simon, 1987.

Bonnycastle, Stephen. "Robertson Davies and the Ethics of Monologue." *Journal of Canadian Studies* 12.1 (1977): 21–40.

_____ . "Structure and Consciousness in Joshua Then and Now." Darling 159–78.

Brainerd, Barron. "An Exploratory Study of Pronouns and Articles as Indices of Genre in English." *Language and Style* 5 (1973): 57–63.

_____ . "On the Distinction between a Novel and a Romance." *Computers and the Humanities* 7 (1973): 259–69.

Bridgman, Richard. *The Colloquial Style in America*. New York: Oxford UP, 1966.

Buckler, Ernest. *The Mountain and the Valley*. New Canadian Library 23. Toronto: McClelland, 1970.

Cain, William E. *The Crisis in Criticism*. Baltimore: Johns Hopkins UP, 1987.

Callaghan, Morley. *A Native Argosy*. New York: Scribner's, 1929.

_____ . *Strange Fugitive*. Edmonton: Hurtig, 1970.

_____ . *That Summer in Paris*. Toronto: Macmillan, 1963.

Chamberlain, John. "Morley Callaghan's Inarticulate People." *The New York Times Book Review* 24 Mar. 1929: 9.

Chomsky, Noam. *Aspects of the Theory of Syntax*. Cambridge, MA: MIT, 1964.

_____ . *Syntactic Structures*. Cambridge, MA: MIT, 1958.

Cluett, Robert. *Prose Style & Critical Reading*. New York: Teachers College, 1976.

_____. "Robertson Davies: The Tory Mode." *Journal of Canadian Studies* 12.1 (1977): 41–46.

_____. "Surface Structures: The Syntactic Profile of Surfacing." Grace and Weir 67–90.

_____, and Suzanne Ives. "An Art of Objects." Darling 139–58.

Cohen, Leonard. *The Favorite Game*. New York: Avon, 1965.

Colie, Rosalie. *The Resources of Kind*. Berkeley: U of California P, 1973.

Connor, Ralph. *The Man from Glengarry: A Tale of the Ottawa*. New York: Grosset, 1906.

Conron, Brandon. *Morley Callaghan*. New York: Twayne, 1966.

Creighton, Donald. *Dominion of the North: A History of Canada*. Rev ed. Toronto: Macmillan, 1957.

Croll, Morris W. *Style, Rhetoric, Rhythm*. Princeton: Princeton UP, 1966.

Cude, Wilfred. *A Due Sense of Difference*. Lanham, MD: UP of America, 1980.

_____. "Historiography and Those Damned Saints: Shadow and Light in *Fifth Business*." *Journal of Canadian Studies*. 12.1 (1977): 48–67.

Darling, Michael, ed. *Perspectives on Mordecai Richler*. Toronto: ECW, 1986.

Davey, Frank. *Margaret Atwood: A Feminist Poetics*. Vancouver: Talon, 1984.

Davidson, Arnold E., and Cathy N. Davidson, ed. *The Art of Margaret Atwood*. Toronto: Anansi, 1981. 177–204.

Davies, Robertson. *Fifth Business*. Bergenfield, NJ: New American Library, 1971.

_____. *The Manticore*. Toronto: Macmillan, 1972.

_____. *A Voice from the Attic*. Toronto: McClelland, 1972.

de la Roche, Mazo. *Jalna*. Toronto: Macmillan, 1927.

Derrida, Jacques. *Of Grammatology*. Baltimore: Johns Hopkins UP, 1976.

Dewart, Rev. E.H. *The Bible under Higher Criticism: A Review of Current Evolution Theories about the Old Testament*. Toronto: Briggs, 1900.

Diefenbaker, John G. *One Canada: Memoirs of the Right Honourable John G. Diefenbaker; Volume 1, The Crusading Years 1895–1956*. Toronto: Macmillan, 1975.

Dobbs, Kildare. *Reading the Time*. Toronto: Macmillan, 1968.

Donow, Herbert S. *A Concordance to the Sonnet Sequences of Daniel, Drayton, Shakespeare, Sidney, and Spenser*. Carbondale: Southern Illinois UP, 1970.

Duncan, Sara Jeannette. *The Imperialist*. New Canadian Library 20. Toronto: McClelland, 1961.

Fish, Stanley. "Interpreting the 'Variorum.'" *Critical Inquiry* 2 (1976): 465–85.

_____. "What Is Stylistics and Why Are They Saying Such Terrible Things About It?" *Approaches to Poetics*. Ed. Seymour Chatman. New York: Columbia UP, 1973. 109–52.

Fries, Charles C. *The Structure of English*. London: Longmans, 1957.

Frye, Northrop. *Fables of Identity: Studies in Poetic Mythology*. New York: Harcourt, 1963.

Fulford, Robert. *Crisis at the Victory Burlesk: Culture, Politics and Other Diversions*. Toronto: Oxford UP, 1968.

Fuller, Edmund. *Man in Modern Fiction*. New York: Random, 1960.

Galbraith, John Kenneth. *The New Industrial State*. New York: New American Library, 1978.

Gerstenberger, Donna. "Conceptions Literary and Otherwise: Women Writers and the Modern Imagination." *Novel: A Forum on Fiction* 9.2 (1976): 141–50.

Gibson, Graeme. *Eleven Canadian Novelists*. Toronto: Anansi, 1973.

Godard, Barbara. "World of Wonders: Robertson Davies' Carnival." *Essays on Canadian Writing* 30 (1984–85): 239–86.

Godfrey, Dave. *The New Ancestors*. Toronto: new, 1970.

Grace, Sherrill E. *Violent Duality: A Study of Margaret Atwood*. Montreal: Véhicule, 1980.

_____ , and Lorraine Weir, ed. *Margaret Atwood: Language, Text and System*. Vancouver: U of British Columbia P, 1983.

Graff, Gerald. *Literature Against Itself: Literary Ideas in Modern Society*. Chicago: U of Chicago P, 1979.

Greenstein, Michael. "Richler's Runners: De-Centauring St. Urbain Street." Darling 15–32.

Gregory, Michael. *Language and Situation*. London: Routledge, 1983.

Grove, Frederick Philip. *Fruits of the Earth*. New Canadian Library 49. Toronto: McClelland, 1965.

Gutwinski, Waldemar. *Cohesion in Literary Texts*. The Hague: Mouton, 1976.

Halliday, M.A.K. *Cohesion in English*. London: Longman, 1976.

_____ . *Introduction to Functional Grammar*. London: E. Arnold, 1985.

_____ . *Language as Social Semiotic*. London: E. Arnold, 1978.

Heintzman, Ralph. "The Virtues of Reverence." *Journal of Canadian Studies* 12.1 (1977): 1–2.

Hemingway, E. *Death in the Afternoon*. New York: Scribner, 1932.

Henderson, J.L.H. *John Strachan: Documents and Opinions*. Carleton Library 44. Toronto: McClelland, 1969.

Hoar, Victor. *Morley Callaghan*. Toronto: Copp Clark, 1969.

Hood, Hugh. *The Swing in the Garden*. Ottawa: Oberon, 1975.

Howe, Joseph. *Poems and Essays*. Toronto: U of Toronto P, 1973.

Hunter, Paul T. *Occasional Form*. Baltimore: Johns Hopkins UP, 1975.

Hutcheon, Linda. "From Poetic to Narrative Structures: The Novels of Margaret Atwood." Grace and Weir 17–32.

Jakobsen, Roman. *Selected Writings*. New York: Columbia UP, 1972.

Keith, W.J. "Canadian Classics." *Canadian Forum* Mar. 1982: 34.

_____ . *Canadian Literature in English*. Harlow, Essex: Longman, 1985.

Laurence, Margaret. *The Stone Angel*. New Canadian Library 59. Toronto: McClelland, 1964.

Layton, Irving. *Engagements: The Prose of Irving Layton*. Ed. Seymour Mayne. Toronto: McClelland, 1972.

Leacock, Stephen. *Sunshine Sketches of a Little Town*. Toronto: Bell, 1912.

_____ . *Sunshine Sketches of a Little Town*. New Canadian Library 15. Toronto: McClelland, 1963.

Lecker, Robert. "Janus through the Looking Glass." Davidson 177–204.

Levin, Harry. "Observations on the Style of Hemingway." *Kenyon Review* 12 (1951): 581–609.

Lowry, Malcolm. *Under the Volcano.* Philadelphia: Lippincott, 1965.

MacLennan, Hugh. *Each Man's Son.* Toronto: Macmillan, 1951.

_____. *Two Solitudes.* Toronto: Collins, 1945.

Mackenzie, William Lyon. *1837: Revolution in the Canadas.* Ed. Greg Keilty. Toronto: NC, 1974.

Mandel, Eli. "Atwood's Poetic Politics." Grace 53–66.

McGee, D'Arcy. *A Collection of Speeches and Addresses.* Ed. Charles Murphy. Toronto: Macmillan, 1937.

McLuhan, Marshall. *The Gutenberg Galaxy: The Making of Typographic Man.* Toronto: U of Toronto P, 1962.

_____. *Understanding Media: The Extensions of Man.* Bergenfield, NJ: New American Library, 1964.

Metcalf, John. "Black Humour: An Interview with Mordecai Richler." *Journal of Canadian Fiction* 3.1 (1974): 73.

Milic, Louis T. *A Quantitative Approach to the Style of Swift.* The Hague: Mouton, 1967.

Mitchell, W.O. *Who Has Seen the Wind.* Toronto: Macmillan, 1976.

Montgomery, Lucy Maud. *Anne of Green Gables.* Toronto: Ryerson, 1964.

Moodie, Susanna. *Roughing It in the Bush; or Forest Life in Canada.* New Canadian Library 31. Toronto: McClelland, 1970.

Morley, Patricia. *Morley Callaghan.* Toronto: McClelland, 1978.

Nelson, William. *The Poetry of Edmund Spenser.* New York: Columbia UP, 1963.

Newman, Peter C. *A Nation Divided: Canada and the Coming of Pierre Trudeau.* New York: Knopf, 1969.

Ostenso, Martha. *Wild Geese.* New York: Dodd, 1925.

Pearson, Lester B. *Mike: The Memoirs of the Right Honourable Lester B. Pearson; Volume 1, 1897-1948.* Toronto: U of Toronto P, 1972.

Peterman, Michael. *Robertson Davies.* Boston: Twayne, 1986.

Peterson, Richard K. *Hemingway Direct and Oblique.* The Hague: Mouton, 1969.

Pike, J.A., A. R. Becker, and J.M. Young. *Language in Relation to a Unified Theory of Human Behavior.* Bloomington: U of Indiana P, 1978.

Pratt, Annis. "Surfacing and the Rebirth Journey." Davidson 139–57.

Randall, John Hermann. *The School of Padua and the Emergence of Modern Science.* New York: Columbia UP, 1933.

Richardson, John. *Wacousta: A Tale of the Pontiac Conspiracy.* Toronto: Mc-Clelland, 1967.

Richler, Mordecai. *The Apprenticeship of Duddy Kravitz.* London: Deutsch, 1959.

_____. *Hunting Tigers Under Glass: Essays and Reports.* Toronto: McClelland, 1968.

Rosenberg, Jerome H. *Margaret Atwood.* Boston: Twayne, 1984.

Ross, Sinclair. *As for Me and My House.* New Canadian Library 4. Toronto: McClelland, 1970.

Roudiez, Leon S., trans. Introduction. *Desire in Language*. By Julia Kristeva. New York: Columbia UP, 1980. 1–20.

Schapiro, Meyer. "Style." *The Problem of Style*. Ed. J.V. Cunningham. Greenwich, CT: Fawcett, 1966.

Shapiro, Michael. *The Sense of Grammar*. Bloomington: Indiana UP, 1983.

Sherman, W.H. *A Handbook of Literary Criticism*. Folcroft PA: Folcroft, 1977.

Spenser, John, and Michael Gregory. "An Approach to the Study of Style." *Linguistics and Literary Style*. Ed. Donald C. Freeman. New York: Holt, 1970.

Sprat, Thomas. *History of the Royal Society*. London: J. Martyn, 1667.

Stein, Gertrude. *The Autobiography of Alice B. Toklas*. New York: Literary Guild, 1933.

Steiner, George. "Literature and Post-History." *Language and Silence*. New York: Atheneum, 1967. 381.

_____ . *A Reader*. Oxford: Oxford UP, 1984.

Stewart, Walter. *Shrug: Trudeau in Power*. Toronto: new, 1971.

Stratford, Philip. "The Uses of Ambiguity: Margaret Atwood and Hubert Aquin." Grace and Weir 113–24.

Strelka, J.P. *Theories of Literary Genre*. University Park, PA: Pennsylvania State UP, 1978.

Tayler, William Edward. *Nature and Art in Renaissance Literature*. New York: Columbia UP, 1964.

Watt, Ian. "The First Paragraph of The Ambassadors: An Explication." *Essays in Stylistic Analysis*. Ed. H.S. Babb. New York: Harcourt, 1972. 275–92.

Weir, Lorraine. "Atwood in a Landscape." Grace and Weir 143–52.

Wiseman, Adele. *The Sacrifice*. New York: Viking, 1956.

Wolf, Leonard. "Defending the New Criticism." Lecture, NDEA English Institute, Columbia University, July 1966.

Woodcock, George. "Lost Eurydice: The Novels of Callaghan." *Canadian Literature* 21.2 (1964): 21–35.

_____ . "Metamorphosis and Survival." Grace and Weir 141.

_____ . *Mordecai Richler*. Canadian Writers 6. Toronto: McClelland, 1970.

_____ . *Odysseus Ever Returning*. New Canadian Library 71. Toronto: McClelland, 1982.

_____ . *The Rejection of Politics and Other Essays on Canada, Canadians, Anarchism and the World*. Toronto: new, 1972.

APPENDIX A: DATA SUMMARY

Key

All word classes are given in Table 1.3, pages 27–78.

+Cl.   Independent clauses added with *and* or *or*.

PL   Period length in words.

1st Sub   Average distance in words from beginning of period to first subordinate clause.

No 42 43   Number of periods with neither subordinator (42) nor relative (43).

IC   Number of independent clauses in the sample.

RSC   Number of rankshifted clauses in the sample.

FRSC   Number of finite rankshifted clauses in the sample.

NFC   Number of nonfinite clauses in the sample.

M   Total number of modifiers: adjectives (03), adverbs (04), intensifiers (33), and function adverbs (34).

//   Incidence of sequences that are *prima facie* evidences of word-parallelism.

D   Number of different three-class (two-digit) sequences in the sample.

N   Number of lexemes and function words in the sample: the total number of items in the sample less the punctuation.

	00	01	02	03	04	05	06	07	11	21	31	32	33	34	35	41	42	43	44	45	51	61	62	71	81	91	97	98	99 + C1	012	017
Strachan	6	761	211	275	80	69	48	37	142	248	550	11	19	66	15	189	69	51	1	8	526	24	71		31	6		4	90	3	3
MacKenzie	13	848	283	197	60	68	39	16	235	193	473	16	8	82	13	196	68	40	2	12	467	16	62	2	54	6	16	20	96	3	15
Moodie	11	811	275	247	53	79	29	31	237	185	534	26	25	78	16	153	50	56		4	471	11	79	3	19	2	4	28	129	13	17
McGee	8	913	191	279	47	45	38	12	138	182	474	13	23	79	22	167	75	29		4	517	23	45		87	5	29	25	99	9	24
Howe	13	795	261	272	34	45	40	12	205	241	475	16	10	62	17	207	80	66	9	4	433	20	42	3	21	8	2	14	103	11	14
Dewart	9	784	259	362	44	43	23	19	134	258	523	6	23	19	27	127	105	69	9	12	472	35	56		3	7	6	3	121	6	1
Creighton	1	989	181	357	53	45	15	13	74	189	533	7	21	61	8	170	27	51	1	9	502	15	51		80	4	28	3	119	34	47
McLuhan I	3	889	160	435	39	52	32	21	68	188	486	10	12	75	14	158	57	35	10	14	507	27	54	1	35	24	28	15	151	18	6
Davies	6	765	272	279	57	40	20	17	228	298	418	9	11	66	33	137	75	74	1	12	412	20	59	4	45	12	20	38	137	19	16
Frye	7	889	237	294	49	35	17	30	161	214	522	17	22	57	21	163	66	81	9	12	487	17	39		26	24	8	12	120	14	35
Callaghan	43	623	369	213	47	48	45	33	384	300	352	56	15	82	29	132	94	33	2	3	340	18	64	5	19	10	14	7	210	18	17
Newman	12	954	261	279	38	62	62	25	123	169	452	25	21	65	13	93	67	32		11	418	9	53		78	2	16	12	148	63	17
McLuhan II	2	945	200	382	61	44	17	47	94	208	449	11	18	75	9	169	64	39	4	16	499	20	49		20	6	4	17	167	35	7
Dobbs	15	881	243	314	70	36	54	18	187	221	420	32	12	75	17	139	57	36			405	27	42	2	49	6	26	20	200	37	19
Berton I	11	946	252	263	40	59	47	22	129	191	488	35	10	55	14	101	63	28	4	2	413	11	64		61	9	12	14	165	36	41
Berton II	8	860	243	287	43	55	29	20	173	254	480	18	18	66	20	112	91	47	8	10	406	30	55	4	55	19	10	12	154	69	18
Fulford	15	776	259	301	70	52	38	26	214	253	418	25	27	63	17	105	63	51	6	8	410	21	61		50	16	50	21	150	32	13
Richler	16	809	247	274	46	49	48	20	206	191	375	25	13	82	25	126	54	36	4	5	353	20	44	15	38	20	24	8	158	72	52
Diefenbaker	10	858	270	230	39	49	46	15	229	233	448	12	15	73	34	116	73	41	1	4	427	23	57		67	11	16	10	171	49	20
Pearson	11	774	258	303	58	68	30	26	244	219	436	16	30	81	17	144	80	27		4	452	22	73		60	20	11	15	158	52	16

	115	211	212	213	214	311	313	411	412	413	035	022	023	995	992	PL	1st Sub	No 43	1C	RSC	FRSC	NFC	M	//	D	N
Strachan	78	65	41	51	86	355	53	170	8	0	28	72	9	4	2	39.1	14.9	30	136	280	126	154	440	121	782	3509
MacKenzie	135	41	36	66	46	256	85	169	12	0	6	44	3	0	2	36.5	15.0	41	228	244	121	123	347	111	862	3457
Moodie	135	47	28	53	55	304	97	127	16	5	16	38	8	1	0	27.3	16.4	60	211	256	117	139	403	65	755	3474
McGee	92	44	33	60	42	298	83	131	14	1	24	29	8	0	1	35.3	17.3	40	139	207	112	95	430	147	861	3424
Howe	133	59	50	77	52	270	77	156	20	1	17	42	5	0	9	33.3	12.7	30	179	256	159	97	378	127	752	3398
Dewart	88	60	36	62	91	372	68	91	17	0	5	90	1	0	3	28.6	7.9	37	138	268	183	85	448	94	689	3432
Creighton	48	46	22	74	44	398	75	140	22	4	15	34	4	0	0	29.3	16.9	60	176	152	79	73	492	145	739	3457
McLuhan I	134	39	14	99	32	341	77	103	16	10	11	24	3	0	1	23.0	9.3	81	167	197	92	105	561	108	802	3418
Davies	151	60	42	118	73	207	119	97	23	1	13	57	7	4	9	25.2	11.0	54	235	232	155	77	413	61	846	3382
Frye	87	30	38	97	45	322	131	109	18	1	16	41	4	2	4	24.5	13.0	38	180	236	154	82	422	102	843	3506
Callaghan	260	112	66	78	44	161	87	96	26	0	11	16	21	5	17	16.2	7.0	121	277	296	170	126	357	58	880	3323
Newman	72	36	37	44	52	254	87	69	15	0	10	33	17	2	3	23.3	9.4	81	194	260	111	149	403	66	839	3396
McLuhan II	63	47	33	87	41	313	86	129	10	0	16	26	3	7	1	20.5	10.2	86	182	213	105	108	536	155	731	3401
Dobbs	118	47	25	97	47	242	78	103	27	3	28	31	14	7	3	17.1	8.0	126	232	216	108	108	471	82	864	3356
Berton I	92	50	28	57	50	331	90	85	11	0	8	38	8	0	0	20.7	10.9	93	207	230	102	128	368	75	763	3372
Berton II	116	39	40	89	75	270	122	82	10	1	20	53	17	1	21	22.4	9.2	73	196	250	146	104	414	78	861	3495
Fulford	124	60	48	80	55	258	81	71	19	1	10	41	13	0	8	23.1	9.0	75	210	245	129	116	461	68	985	3367
Richler	132	41	31	76	42	187	123	87	14	3	21	29	27	11	5	20.2	8.0	104	217	223	106	117	415	88	992	3160
Diefenbaker	173	38	65	69	59	242	111	79	16	0	15	52	7	0	2	19.9	8.8	102	215	234	124	110	357	84	835	3371
Pearson	173	43	43	75	54	310	87	104	14	0	16	39	15	1	0	22.4	11.7	93	215	242	118	124	472	84	884	3450

	00	01	02	03	04	05	06	07	11	21	31	32	33	34	35	41	42	43	44	45	51	61	62	71	81	91	97	98	99 +CL	012	012	017
Woodcock I	4	900	207	374	38	43	35	32	103	180	480	10	34	73	21	156	57	64		5	529	20	49		33	19	25	5	105	20	17	33
Galbraith	6	821	233	305	70	54	23	39	126	280	465	10	31	45	19	136	70	49		8	414	22	58		23	18	21	11	183	12	29	2
Layton	18	806	253	272	61	67	34	23	211	247	451	22	38	61	34	143	79	53	4	20	392	18	62	1	12	30	10	29	138	16	27	9
Woodcock II	11	867	251	347	68	32	28	42	167	186	493	12	24	64	19	127	53	74	2	12	474	19	39		24	19	6	28	131	24	26	48
Atwood	14	804	253	265	40	32	47	23	215	262	417	10	20	96	21	145	45	46	1	18	391	19	39		16	12	74	73	122	24	27	34
Stewart	8	941	235	281	60	55	45	22	161	207	408	21	18	62	20	129	46	40	1	2	429	9	59		87	11	48	30	125	22	66	20
Connor	4	781	301	250	58	47	65	16	192	138	472	28	12	107	16	189	67	42		9	423	18	47		24	3	3	2	139	61	9	3
Duncan	15	829	255	264	65	47	47	9	220	263	506	10	31	72	23	112	51	57		12	582	14	59		12	8	9	41	124	35	20	13
Montgomery	14	870	295	368	68	41	55	13	198	176	418	21	22	109	24	156	65	43		2	431	7	46	2	10	4	27	24	134	40	35	10
Leacock I	11	761	293	204	36	36	36	22	290	236	434	12	10	104	28	162	117	35	4	6	445	31	44	7	33	18	12	9	148	43	24	5
Leacock II	19	741	310	166	52	40	33	15	291	257	469	30	15	107	38	155	120	30	2		385	25	39	9	33	16	23	20	147	36	35	15
Ostenso	11	791	308	240	48	43	49	14	214	236	470	26	21	93	33	133	53	42	1	2	415	21	40	3	21	2	5	27	206	37	21	9
de la Roche	10	752	284	319	63	39	65	7	252	189	465	18	20	98	9	129	68	29	3		388	11	46	2	40	6	8	15	182	33	15	15
Callaghan	23	717	375	232	81	33	97	21	309	169	467	52	25	94	20	178	52	13			351	10	35	10	31	6	0	3	192	52	36	6
Grove	5	856	337	204	55	33	74	29	191	213	488	36	10	79	19	121	46	44	1	4	460	13	36	3	60	1	4	40	206	33	15	9
Richardson	21	757	261	271	64	47	84	22	168	200	571	7	25	95	16	157	52	78		6	515	10	55	1	14	11	9	18	94	20	8	14

	115	211	212	213	214	311	313	411	412	413	035	022	023	995	992	PL	1st Sub	No 42 43	IC	RSC	FRSC	NFC	M	//	D	N
Woodcock I	72	30	34	74	38	321	88	114	18	4	14	35	2	0	0	33.4	13.7	36	170	235	125	110	519	93	859	3468
Galbraith	94	52	53	101	70	294	93	95	12	0	5	61	6	1	2	18.2	7.4	102	209	241	125	116	451	100	795	3329
Layton	113	53	49	103	41	265	92	106	12	0	12	32	11	2	6	25.1	11.2	56	206	274	150	124	432	117	917	3404
Woodcock II	99	33	23	88	37	287	89	101	14	2	7	27	7	0	5	27.0	13.8	55	187	240	138	102	503	81	843	3473
Atwood	125	44	23		68	235	96	58	23	0	21	37	22	1	1	28.4	15.0	64	249	207	105	102	421	99	970	3396
Stewart	143	44	31	68	62	237	93	102	20	0	2	50	12	0	0	28.1	12.1	65	209	216	94	122	421	117	820	3391
Connor	117	31	23	53	28	239	58	148	30	5	20	19	11	0	0	23.8	11.9	66	241	241	113	128	422	78	813	3302
Duncan	125	45	65	79	68	318	105	79	19	0	21	52	7	1	2	28.4	12.3	63	231	226	123	103	432	58	854	3455
Montgomery	115	39	40	50	43	231	91	132	14	5	26	28	8	1	2	26.3	13.2	68	223	231	122	109	567	92	844	3447
Leacock I	182	59	52	94	27	300	78	116	21	1	20	13	15	1	5	23.3	8.4	64	224	257	163	94	354	73	886	3412
Leacock II	173	61	65	81	43	302	105	124	17	1	20	31	20	5	2	23.4	11.4	64	226	257	169	88	340	63	871	3381
Ostenso	120	48	85	67	35	298	81	116	13	0	18	14	13	6	2	16.3	9.1	138	269	212	106	106	402	54	769	3320
de la Roche	155	34	37	66	50	201	123	104	20	5	21	32	9	3	3	18.3	10.8	114	243	218	107	111	500	76	764	3303
Callaghan	208	51	18	48	49	283	75	153	21	0	14	22	29	4	0	17.7	14.5	141	335	239	88	151	432	82	800	3378
Grove	132	54	35	45	74	284	117	83	27	4	21	56	15	1	4	16.8	9.8	135	287	231	95	136	348	55	783	3443
Richardson	104	67	25	47	55	377	66	104	22	1	12	46	3	0	0	37.4	16.6	26	157	304	151	153	455	56	802	3469

	00	01	02	03	04	05	06	07	11	21	31	32	33	34	35	41	42	43	44	45	51	61	62	71	81	91	97	98	99+CL	012	017
Ross	50	615	349	218	36	51	48	19	383	239	365	30	17	121	32	169	82	38		2	332	32	66	3	9	12	8	25	180	24	1
MacLennan I	47	741	332	215	63	46	65	7	321	223	476	16	18	111	17	130	75	24		2	396	18	47		30		3	9	212	20	5
Lowry	19	805	249	253	57	26	76	12	206	235	469	21	26	131	29	138	37	32	17	2	411	26	35	7	28	12	30	48	163	15	70
Mitchell	7	878	289	228	51	43	51	19	217	183	490	35	11	79	13	100	52	36	3		470	19	39	2	46	7	16	41	152	47	5
MacLennan II	24	725	326	222	40	41	56	19	230	181	455	22	16	118	14	138	85	26	2	2	349	22	40	2	22	6	0	2	159	23	3
Buckler	35	776	311	213	28	38	40	19	296	227	535	34	16	125	27	119	85	30		2	432	16	36		16	3	22	8	179	40	13
Wiseman	13	665	377	175	59	71	47	17	330	283	405	34	23	136	43	115	122	45	12		345	27	71	2	7	6	8	21	211	13	13
Richler	18	831	339	230	90	56	33	11	262	207	394	33	20	76	26	174	61	16	2		320	19	54	3	81	25	18	8	195	62	11
Godfrey	20	810	302	262	34	43	52	15	296	218	395	14	25	115	39	113	73	37	8	3	361	16	49	9	36	10	3	30	294	39	47
Hood	8	917	225	284	45	48	51	11	217	183	453	22	15	122	33	125	58	27			464	13	48	2	35	3	26	12	167	67	58
Davies I	22	715	300	242	74	43	36	22	331	250	426	20	18	87	28	170	87	48	4	2	379	16	50	3	36	7	14	24	127	25	14
Cohen	24	747	341	264	39	42	43	13	341	216	461	24	15	81	47	106	52	33	5	4	356	20	45	3	19	2	0	5	251	33	7
Laurence	26	649	368	232	43	31	56	16	384	283	383	43	15	137	56	173	57	25	13	2	308	21	38	7	12	5	14	9	235	17	18
Atwood I	43	646	337	215	19	43	75	9	433	280	413	27	8	97	37	146	62	29	2	2	330	22	46	1	9	4	6	52	140	30	38
Davies II	25	634	309	200	55	37	23	36	386	326	374	19	21	102	43	159	110	60	8	5	364	18	61	2	23	5	4	20	152	14	14
Atwood II	43	736	319	267	20	48	60	27	331	241	387	19	11	113	33	71	55	31	1	2	356	17	62		22	6	39	32	217	49	39
Atwood III	31	657	319	262	35	52	51	24	330	257	425	20	7	146	28	127	46	33	7	7	379	17	67	1	24	4	3	36	174	33	17

	115	211	212	213	214	311	313	411	412	413	035	022	023	995	992	PL	1st Sub	No 42 43	IC	RSC	FRSC	NFC	M	//	D	N
Ross	237	36	58	102	40	143	123	128	31	2	20	9	18	5	0	18.6	10.3	94	281	288	170	118	392	67	915	3275
MacLennan I	202	67	32	95	36	211	103	103	22	14	19	20	6	4	4	16.2	7.6	137	281	264	146	118	397	56	761	3375
Lowry	121	71	31	67	63	292	89	86	28	5	25	15	38	9	21	21.1	16.0	115	228	202	88	114	467	77	895	3341
Mitchell	147	64	37	61	20	287	82	77	13	3	15	8	6	2	7	22.5	10.7	93	255	208	95	113	369	73	742	3361
MacLennan II	150	42	34	70	33	257	78	118	14	3	13	15	17	0	2	20.0	10.8	75	261	242	135	107	496	52	716	3151
Buckler	178	53	60	78	35	351	81	89	22	0	17	24	13	0	0	19.5	8.8	108	238	248	151	97	382	50	770	3425
Wiseman	199	104	51	77	51	216	68	90	22	1	13	24	15	5	16	16.4	7.4	114	274	313	180	133	396	45	862	3418
Richler	176	44	37	82	40	191	117	147	20	1	23	29	9	5	1	17.3	11.0	129	326	195	95	100	376	90	867	3327
Godfrey	180	58	64	61	27	209	80	76	23	2	24	19	13	87	16	11.6	8.3	227	233	240	130	110	436	70	834	3344
Hood	146	30	67	59	59	306	99	83	25	1	21	30	12	2		20.7	9.7	88	191	203	93	110	467	113	833	3388
Davies I	230	61	37	97	48	205	112	125	30	3	13	34	4	2	5	27.4	13.8	50	240	258	157	101	431	87	900	3412
Cohen	226	48	34	83	49	243	102	81	13	0	22	21	24	8	5	13.4	7.4	180	315	207	109	98	399	54	720	3323
Laurence	251	87	81	83	32	195	81	126	24	7	16	25	14	7	17	14.5	10.2	170	343	211	108	103	427	73	839	3362
Atwood	291	61	66	100	50	225	103	108	25	0	21	26	22	10	1	24.8	11.3	76	303	261	134	127	339	72	716	3297
Davies II	238	82	62	125	49	150	106	103	29	2	14	31	12	4	15	22.7	10.1	58	239	291	195	96	378	59	924	3389
Atwood II	202	78	44	69	48	208	73	41	12	0	20	27	27	28	3	15.5	7.9	152	259	263	129	134	411	39	795	3248
Atwood III	222	70	55	72	60	204	116	80	20	0	18	36	18	2	6	19.6	12.3	117	281	237	110	127	450	50	770	3336

185

	00	01	02	03	04	05	06	07	11	21	31	32	33	34	35	41	42	43	44	45	51	61	62	71	81	91	97	98	99	012	017
Hawthorne	5	693	275	275	69	58	50	29	228	195	437	7	20	127	18	181	103	55	2	9	435	7	55	1	23	12	19	22	98	16	5
Howells	18	645	296	239	72	70	52	15	325	246	440	4	21	93	44	155	115	53	0	4	439	21	65	0	13	3	3	44	99	10	5
Twain	56	455	373	165	52	63	44	21	451	233	341	106	12	180	62	290	72	20	1	2	230	38	57	7	41	7	0	36	111	12	3
James	40	687	301	266	57	45	14	25	310	315	425	20	35	108	33	109	101	55	3	10	389	26	49	1	4	21	12	42	113	12	22
Fitzgerald	5	901	239	321	49	34	49	14	190	167	519	28	10	98	13	142	41	41	1	4	482	21	34	5	43	12	12	26	140	56	20
Steinbeck	8	773	395	204	64	35	33	9	244	168	464	43	13	130	18	191	59	34	2	0	335	18	39	1	33	3	3	3	206	37	21
West	7	765	410	185	25	81	21	33	349	172	445	29	28	62	15	135	79	31	1	2	315	10	90	1	17	1	1	1	259	38	24
Faulkner	21	628	332	225	32	39	86	25	367	229	389	72	16	123	50	203	117	22	0	0	369	23	46	0	24	10	0	12	152	17	7
Nabokov	22	841	229	365	58	38	61	17	176	152	489	20	17	82	15	111	58	26	1	2	413	12	43	7	25	8	39	24	119	74	32
Roth	22	704	283	211	67	39	63	13	320	241	418	36	23	117	34	155	65	51	0	2	361	18	55	14	29	9	35	30	153	41	14

	115	211	212	213	214	311	313	411	412	413	035	022	023	995	992	PL	1st Sub	IC	RSC	FRSC	NFC	M	//	D	N	No 42 43
Hawthorne	137	57	33	53	49	214	85	145	21	0	14	34	9	0	3	34.8	13.1	165	300	163	137	491	66	923	3366	21
Howells	197	87	47	79	31	232	56	120	24	0	12	23	8	0	0	35.3	13.4	189	323	186	137	415	59	911	3421	24
Twain	279	43	67	86	35	168	82	241	28	2	32	11	20	1	0	30.8	18.0	311	276	148	128	409	62	929	3325	59
James	180	114	68	86	42	212	109	75	23	5	10	36	9	1	3	31.0	12.1	191	280	196	84	466	34	912	3412	32
Fitzgerald	115	31	22	81	30	279	112	113	16	3	19	16	9	2	2	25.0	12.9	233	184	87	97	478	100	791	3458	78
Steinbeck	158	33	41	57	37	272	105	171	5	0	3	13	19	0	2	16.2	7.7	351	178	101	77	411	80	730	3308	135
West	246	58	19	59	29	218	98	101	28	2	20	22	16	0	2	12.8	4.6	352	252	117	135	300	73	694	3314	164
Faulkner	211	64	50	80	33	255	70	173	22	0	42	11	25	5	0	22.8	9.2	252	310	160	150	396	57	920	3430	85
Nabokov	115	62	29	31	25	225	132	91	11	1	11	14	11	23	5	28.8	18.0	154	222	106	116	522	71	876	3343	68
Roth	201	67	49	77	43	217	92	125	12	0	22	13	22	16	34	22.6	13.2	222	253	138	115	418	66	1000	3376	82

187

	00	01	02	03	04	05	06	07	11	21	31	32	33	34	35	41	42	43	44	45	51	61	62	71	81	91	97	98	99	012	017
Cooper	13	732	241	291	70	64	28	22	153	273	537	8	33	73	23	127	80	58	1	2	445	34	72	1	32	16	4	16	128	10	1
Jefferson	6	794	239	216	37	58	53	27	171	242	537	16	15	61	17	123	64	63	3	3	537	8	73	0	27	19	1	17	81	9	11
Thoreau	7	679	269	248	71	57	61	23	269	228	477	24	31	119	33	199	97	50	13	2	380	25	54	3	23	16	8	38	112	24	6
Mencken	21	732	225	346	115	40	27	27	247	225	471	25	53	69	25	164	63	37	5	21	432	27	51	5	21	15	8	17	147	25	3
Stein	15	621	359	199	77	26	24	10	367	339	373	27	24	176	54	203	100	51	4	0	244	57	43	11	31	14	0	0	121	26	28
Hemingway	20	752	265	218	49	54	42	21	255	253	503	16	20	101	24	174	93	47	1	17	403	26	54	0	40	9	0	5	121	17	9
Fitzgerald	20	728	255	265	33	45	46	14	225	284	446	29	19	89	18	123	57	31	8	7	390	29	45	8	48	8	27	34	145	51	5
Wilson	6	768	202	292	70	55	18	38	164	225	438	17	32	97	15	158	64	62	2	15	471	19	67	0	25	19	12	38	90	10	19
Stone	18	844	247	295	55	47	30	15	128	202	485	27	24	73	11	93	63	45	4	43	415	13	54	0	54	4	13	5	171	46	23
Didion	19	769	309	198	30	59	37	18	277	234	386	27	21	115	37	165	71	47	6	13	329	27	56	0	46	13	29	24	157	57	45

	115	211	212	213	214	311	313	411	412	413	035	022	023	995	992	PL	1st Sub	IC	RSC	FRSC	NFC	M	//	D	N	No. 42 43
Cooper	80	54	54	78	86	305	105	94	13	1	12	79	3	0	1	27.0	10.8	168	265	151	114	467	63	792	3419	48
Jefferson	188	63	43	27	108	311	71	100	6	0	10	90	3	1	4	43.0	13.1	133	271	133	138	319	50	757	3458	23
Thoreau	164	60	42	80	43	311	103	140	22	1	16	33	5	2	11	31.3	12.5	195	295	154	141	470	85	958	3456	42
Mencken	142	32	41	112	33	239	109	124	23	1	3	30	1	2	5	24.0	10.9	216	215	121	94	583	77	929	3475	85
Stein	242	73	54	148	54	183	121	156	37	0	18	40	12	2	0	28.6	12.9	342	226	166	60	476	59	1000	3446	47
Hemingway	171	62	38	106	44	309	96	117	23	2	20	39	8	1	0	28.0	11.3	211	277	160	117	388	87	918	3451	45
Fitzgerald	148	50	33	69	31	265	116	99	19	1	7	24	10	11	3	22.3	12.9	216	213	108	105	406	50	804	3147	48
Wilson	85	63	27	82	49	267	71	125	18	1	17	26	17	0	6	34.8	14.4	152	243	132	111	491	83	912	3335	32
Stone	89	36	27	75	60	309	98	68	15	0	18	51	5	1	4	19.5	10.8	196	218	126	92	447	64	841	3264	96
Didion	188	64	35	94	40	232	89	128	31	0	17	14	21	1	6	21.9	13.1	266	251	137	114	364	69	1000	3349	88

	00	01	02	03	04	05	06	07	11	21	31	32	33	34	35	41	42	43	44	45	51	61	62	71	81	91	97	98	99	012	017
Huxley	3	738	222	289	58	57	27	45	193	268	462	20	18	68	21	135	84	66	3	10	491	30	70	0	14	15	16	27	97	25	6
Arnold	2	734	194	369	62	70	25	19	208	263	462	8	26	73	45	144	62	45	5	2	453	31	78	1	28	19	16	47	119	7	12
Conrad	5	745	201	288	75	44	27	12	255	228	542	11	23	69	40	118	56	56	1	18	496	13	46	2	34	10	10	17	146	18	18
Joyce	2	839	240	330	51	26	30	10	181	226	508	11	27	86	20	175	83	58	1	5	468	28	36	2	12	7	17	10	118	11	15
Woolf	7	765	288	250	51	64	38	17	220	253	468	24	32	67	25	155	85	60	9	12	390	33	64	8	22	18	2	28	150	15	15
Forster	10	750	300	248	69	34	22	17	291	303	440	21	17	100	44	159	74	54	7	3	374	12	47	7	12	7	13	29	164	6	21
Waugh	10	825	266	279	59	31	43	8	244	243	448	6	8	88	19	146	50	41	3	8	452	19	39	0	42	4	19	22	171	41	11
Orwell	10	828	244	278	68	25	30	20	183	264	421	13	24	93	37	122	76	50	3	2	417	14	48	0	36	20	34	14	150	35	25
Burgess	11	912	202	332	52	50	33	29	149	229	444	16	30	65	25	149	49	47	0	6	433	29	60	1	22	19	42	33	118	43	53
Steiner	4	868	203	415	45	40	25	19	138	192	444	11	30	62	16	166	54	41	9	12	449	16	47	0	26	12	16	16	168	20	16

	115	211	212	213	214	311	313	411	412	413	035	022	023	995	992	PL	1st Sub	IC	RSC	FRSC	NFC	M	//	D	N	No 42 43
Huxley	113	43	65	90	63	319	67	89	20	5	12	57	1	0	4	35.5	11.5	159	279	153	129	433	58	867	3421	22
Arnold	102	61	52	98	55	284	80	95	30	1	23	41	6	1	6	29.4	14.6	183	223	109	114	530	80	836	3480	57
Conrad	157	45	48	101	32	282	101	74	19	9	12	31	1	7	2	23.5	12.1	185	200	117	83	455	66	791	3412	73
Joyce	98	44	33	88	61	304	94	142	15	2	11	59	6	0	0	29.6	12.0	185	209	143	66	494	108	801	3460	44
Woolf	138	51	45	110	44	275	78	101	23	5	6	36	10	0	6	23.1	10.6	246	271	152	119	400	60	920	3424	74
Forster	188	51	67	130	46	255	87	114	26	2	19	43	0	7	8	21.3	12.2	292	211	138	73	434	77	840	3432	76
Waugh	170	54	20	105	60	212	99	110	20	1	14	57	3	1	7	20.0	12.7	270	183	101	82	434	77	801	3371	105
Orwell	133	59	42	115	41	207	125	80	27	0	4	32	9	0	3	22.2	11.1	223	231	136	75	463	78	938	3333	73
Burgess	86	38	34	107	47	280	100	95	35	0	14	41	1	0	3	26.4	12.8	202	219	107	112	479	128	904	3387	56
Steiner	90	28	35	89	35	263	93	113	26	1	21	31	3	0	0	20.4	9.9	193	183	99	84	552	134	805	3384	97

	00	01	02	03	04	05	06	07	11	21	31	32	33	34	35	41	42	43	44	45	51	61	62	71	81	91	97	98	99	012	017
Dickens	11	700	266	241	72	60	39	24	280	246	444	6	18	96	23	181	107	33	5	0	450	23	62	9	21	10	12	31	107	24	8
Trollope	8	729	262	234	61	60	42	12	225	283	469	19	23	72	29	148	88	36	5	4	416	16	62	8	25	11	12	44	99	11	11
Stevenson	25	655	308	196	82	46	53	11	337	192	469	41	38	113	15	186	92	45	2	12	434	18	54	0	15	10	12	49	107	13	5
Conrad	3	886	219	378	66	28	55	19	148	197	510	26	35	65	32	120	40	37	3	15	505	15	34	0	18	9	23	33	153	18	11
Joyce	5	783	273	262	34	52	43	8	242	221	502	30	14	91	12	202	56	31	10	0	415	30	47	1	33	1	0	22	186	20	5
Lawrence	17	740	273	369	61	19	28	24	287	210	435	28	40	128	26	180	38	33	8	0	355	15	27	4	13	5	0	22	208	36	29
Woolf	15	657	326	197	82	51	77	16	327	251	421	48	18	126	17	155	78	29	1	0	352	37	54	7	17	9	38	41	170	18	12
Forster	14	732	357	211	68	48	33	19	325	263	443	27	11	85	42	181	78	41	3	8	323	19	51	6	14	4	1	40	169	14	18
Orwell	4	778	260	278	85	40	40	26	203	259	489	33	15	122	22	140	68	41	0	2	439	32	46	0	34	4	4	5	176	28	8
Burgess	8	842	236	309	59	18	77	12	208	187	429	30	9	92	20	143	39	22	5	2	390	14	26	11	23	4	21	20	177	60	21

	115	211	212	213	214	311	313	411	412	413	035	022	023	995	992	PL	1st Sub	IC	RSC	FRSC	NFC	M	//	D	N	No 43
Dickens	156	57	43	75	58	214	90	147	19	0	8	45	10	4	5	32.7	13.6	190	274	151	123	427	71	862	3418	45
Trollope	127	73	57	72	86	270	76	114	19	2	28	79	4	0	4	34.6	14.6	202	246	132	114	390	63	863	3362	43
Stevenson	212	50	34	71	29	228	119	153	23	0	11	13	13	0	2	32.8	13.5	217	272	162	110	429	41	906	3426	30
Conrad	100	43	47	66	33	257	136	91	18	3	14	47	3	0	2	23.0	11.0	205	182	80	102	544	79	828	3463	96
Joyce	163	53	25	98	43	302	93	168	29	0	16	22	21	6	11	18.2	11.8	299	195	92	1.3	401	78	703	3406	125
Lawrence	294	41	36	85	43	207	106	139	30	4	44	15	25	14	9	16.3	7.7	270	159	88	71	598	87	787	3347	156
Woolf	200	80	51	83	34	246	78	120	24	0	23	17	18	5	12	20.3	12.5	287	266	122	144	401	60	940	3361	108
Forster	198	68	60	83	47	237	95	126	41	0	23	36	13	2	8	20.4	12.1	307	233	133	100	375	72	842	3386	98
Orwell	129	65	33	83	71	237	131	100	16	0	12	47	18	0	0	19.7	11.4	230	219	113	106	500	73	865	3458	105
Burgess	147	55	21	66	41	213	116	102	23	0	18	22	15	17	7	18.5	11.3	233	176	69	107	469	100	761	3226	131

APPENDIX B: STAFF
YORK COMPUTER INVENTORY
OF PROSE STYLE, 1970–89

PROGRAMMERS
Dr. G.J. Carpenter
Richard Levine
Patricia Mallon
Mary Lea Serpell

ANALYSTS
Linda C. Blom
Tan Ping Chan
Louise M. Drescher
Alison Hope
Suzanne Ives
Joan Laurence
Marie-José Souche
Nancy E. Wright

GRAPHIC DESIGNERS
Leslie Gaskin
Carolyn Gonder
Nathan Mondrowitz
Carol Randall
Robert Ryan
Judith Saul

TRANSLATORS
Linda C. Blom
Derek Dalton
Louise M. Drescher
Eva Epstein
Judith Fitzgerald
Tom Greenwald
Joan Laurence
Anthony Quarrington
Jayne Patterson
Jan Poole
Michael Rehner
Colin Rutledge

EDITORS
Linda C. Blom
Joan Laurence
Lydia Rett
Linda Revie

TYPISTS
Lorraine McLeod
Janice Pearson

APPENDIX C: THE YORK
INVENTORY PROGRAM

The Program of the York Computer Inventory of Prose Style is in fact a series of programs totalling 2200 statements in Fortran IV for the G Compiler. Those programs deal with the parse only of a text, and the parse is delivered in card form: for each 80-column card there are eight digits of identification (four for the sample number, four for the card number of that sample) and seventy-two digits of information. Those 72 digits give coded translation of 24 items — words and/or major punctuation. After reading and printing out the parse of the sample (roughly 150 cards), the programs deliver ten blocks of information about the parse, as listed below.

1. A frequency-ordered list of all three-digit codes in the text, as follows:

PRINTOUT   EXPLANATION (not given on printout)

329 19 9.99   There are 329 nouns used as prepositional phrase completives
235 311 7.13   totalling 9.99% of the text; there are 235 definite determiners
194 511 5.89   totalling 7.13% of the text; there are 194 prepositions heading
191 514 5.80   noun-modifying prepositional phrases; there are 191 preposi-
etc.   tions heading adverbially used prepositional phrases . . .

2. A frequently-ordered list of all two-digit codes in the text, as follows:

804 1 24.41   There are 804 nouns of all kinds, totalling 24.41% of the text;
417 31 12.66   there are 416 determiners of all kinds totalling 12.66% of the text;
391 51 11.87   there are 391 prepositions of all kinds, totalling 11.87% of the
265 3 8.04   text; there are 265 adjectives of all kinds, totalling 8.04% of the
                    text.

3. A count of certain specified sequences of prepositional phrases:

51 01 51   21   There are 21 sequences like this ("in houses at").
51 07 51   0   There are no sequences like this ("by going to").
51 11 51   5   There are 5 sequences like this ("to those of").
51 31 01 51   35   There are 35 sequences like this ("in the house of").

4. The "D" Value, followed by a frequency-ordered list of all 3-class sequences in the sample:

970 3 WD Patterns   The D Value for the sample is 970.

116	51 31 01	There are 116 patterns preposition-determiner-noun.
85	31 01 51	There are 85 patterns determiner-noun-preposition.
81	01 51 31	There are 81 patterns noun-preposition-determiner.

5. A frequency-ordered list of all the three-class sequences that begin sentences:

8	31 01 21	There are 8 openings determiner-noun-auxiliary.
6	31 01 51	There are 6 openings determiner-noun-preposition.
6	31 03 01	There are 6 openings determiner-adjective-noun.

6. A frequency-ordered list of all the three-class sequences that end sentences:

9	51 31 01	There are 9 closings preposition-determiner-noun.
8	01 51 01	There are 8 closings noun-preposition-noun.
4	06 51 01	There are 4 closings participle-preposition-noun.

7. A count of 48 specified word sequences that are prima facie evidences of word-parallelism:

1 1 1	6	There are 6 sequences noun-noun-noun.
1 41 1	24	There are 24 sequences noun-coordinator-noun.
1 41 3	5	There are 5 sequences noun-coordinator-adjective.
1 41 31	17	There are 17 sequences noun-coordinator-determiner.

8. A computation of Pearson's r (reliability coefficient) for all the odd cards in the sample measured against all the even cards in the sample. The purpose of this computation is to measure the sample's internal stability. Samples that produce an r of less than .99 are deemed unstable.

9. Sentence x-Ray. It lists sentences by their number in the text (1,2,3 etc.) and gives for each the following information: Length, word at which the first

pattern-maker occurs (class 61), word at which the first subordinator occurs (class 42), word at which the first relative occurs (class 43), the total number (N) of subordinators, the total number of relatives, and the total number of rankshifted nonfinite constructions (classes 05, 06, 07):

SENTENCE	LENGTH	D61	D42	D43	N42	N43	N567
1	18	0	0	0	0	0	1
2	15	0	0	0	0	0	1
3	32	0	0	0	0	0	2
4	7	0	0	0	0	0	0
5	18	0	0	8	0	1	0

After listing all the sentences in the sample, the program computes the mean per sentence for all categories from length through number of nonfinites (N567), and gives a count of the number of sentences with neither a subordinator (42) nor a relative (43).

10. Noun phrase analysis. This program reads the parse backwards; at each noun it picks up that noun, together with all its attributive modification; it then makes a frequency-ordered list of all the phrases:

244	1 31	There are 244 phrases determiner-noun.
234	1	There are 234 freestanding nouns.
59	1 3 31	There are 59 phrases determiner-adjective-noun.
43	1 3	There are 43 phrases adjective-noun.
26	1 1	There are 26 phrases noun-noun

APPENDIX D: GLOSSARY

DETERMINER: What the old schoolbook grammars called an article, plus the possessive pronouns his, her, its, their. In Fries's grammar, a word that signals the beginning of a noun phrase. Of interest in the study of style as a register of specificity (as in James and Hemingway) or of a high level of generalization (as in Jonson and Johnson and Davies).

EMBEDDED: Used to designate medially placed adverbial elements, usually between subject and predicator. Sidney and Carlyle were great embedders.

FINITE VERB: A verb phrase head that is ended (i.e. finite) for tense, mood, number, person, voice, and aspect. The phrases of such verbs will be predicators of independent, subordinate, and relative clauses.

FUNCTION WORD: One of the two great phyla of English words (Cf. lexeme), consisting of an inelastic stock of roughly 150 words, largely uninflected, that require context in order to "mean." (See code list, App. C).

HYPOTAXIS: Subordinated arrangement of clauses; complex sentences are hypotactic. One might contrast the hypotactic style of either Davies or Ross with the paratactic style of W.O. Mitchell or Malcolm Lowry.

LEFT-BRANCH: A sentence with subordinate elements, especially adverbial elements, at the left, preceding subject and predicator, is said to be left-branched. (Cf. embedded, right-branch)

LEXEME: One of the two great phyla of words, in this case the "content" words known as nouns, verbs, adjectives, and adverbs. All the lexemes are susceptible of inflection, and their stock (at roughly a million items) is theoretically infinite, with old lexemes leaving and new ones entering the language every week, perhaps every day. (Cf. Function Word).

MINUS-ADDITION: Elliptical adding of clauses, especially of independent clauses in compound sentences, most often used to indicate a subjectless second independent clause in a compound sentence: "Jane packed up her things and went home." (The subject, Jane, is not repeated for the second clause).

NONFINITE VERB: A verb phrase that is not ended (i.e. nonfinite) for mood, aspect, number, or person. In short, what is often called a "verbal." The phrases of such verbs will be predicators of participial, gerund, and infinitive clauses.

PARATAXIS: Setting things beside each other in a series of two or more without an

198

explicit subordinate or superordinate relationship. All the forms of parallelism are paratactic, most notably serial use of independent clauses.

RANKSHIFT: In a grammar that offers ranks at four levels (sentence, clause, phrase, word), the term refers to clauses that are subordinated to other clauses or phrases and to phrases subordinated to other phrases or words. In this book, the use of the term always refers to rankshifted clauses: subordinate, relative, participial, gerund, and infinitive.

RIGHT-BRANCH: A sentence with subordinate elements, especially subordinate and relative clauses, at the end, or right-hand side, is said to be right-branched. (Cf. embedded, left-branch).

INDEX